W9-ABX-804

FIRST
PEOPLES
of NORTH
AMERICA

THE PEOPLE AND CULTURE OF THE
MENOMINEE

RAYMOND BIAL

Cavendish
Square

New York

Published in 2016 by Cavendish Square Publishing, LLC
243 5th Avenue, Suite 136, New York, NY 10016

Copyright © 2016 by Cavendish Square Publishing, LLC

First Edition

No part of this publication may be reproduced, stored in a retrieval system, or transmitted in any form or by any means—electronic, mechanical, photocopying, recording, or otherwise—without the prior permission of the copyright owner. Request for permission should be addressed to Permissions, Cavendish Square Publishing, 243 5th Avenue, Suite 136, New York, NY 10016. Tel (877) 980-4450; fax (877) 980-4454.

Website: cavendishsq.com

This publication represents the opinions and views of the author based on his or her personal experience, knowledge, and research. The information in this book serves as a general guide only. The author and publisher have used their best efforts in preparing this book and disclaim liability rising directly or indirectly from the use and application of this book.

CPSIA Compliance Information: Batch #CW16CSQ

All websites were available and accurate when this book was sent to press.

Library of Congress Cataloging-in-Publication Data

Bial, Raymond.
[Menominee.]
The people and culture of the Menominee / Raymond Bial.
pages cm. — (First peoples of North America)
Includes bibliographical references and index.
ISBN 978-1-5026-1002-7 (hardcover) ISBN 978-1-5026-1003-4 (ebook)
1. Menominee Indians—History—Juvenile literature.
2. Menominee Indians—Social life and customs—Juvenile literature. I. Title.

E99.M44B59 2015
977.4004'97313—dc23

2015025192

Editorial Director: David McNamara
Editor: Kristen Susienka
Copy Editor: Nathan Heidelberger
Art Director: Jeffrey Talbot
Designer: Amy Greenan
Senior Production Manager: Jennifer Ryder-Talbot
Production Editor: Renni Johnson
Photo Research: J8 Media

The photographs in this book are used by permission and through the courtesy of: MPI/Getty Images, cover; Marilyn Angel Wynn/Getty Images, back cover, 2, 15, 43, 48, 61, 68, 75; Rick Wilking/Reuters/Newscom, 6; Jeffrey Phelps/Getty Images, 11; Raymond Bail, 13, 16, 24, 91; Marilyn Angel Wynn/Native Stock, 14, 30, 33, 52–53, 67, 69, 83, 98; Charles Cook/Getty Images, 20; CJ Lippert/File:1825 Prairie du Chien Line.jpg/Wikimedia Commons, 22; Photograph Courtesy: Menominee Tribal Historic Preservation Office, 25, 28, 103, 104, 106; Fototeca Gilardi/Getty Images, 29; Public Domain/Charles Bird King/File:Amiskquew.jpg/Wikimedia Commons, 37; Henry L. Batterman Fund and the Frank Sherman Benson Fund/Brooklyn Museum/File:Ball-headed War Club with Spike, early 19th century, 50.67.61.jpg/Wikimedia Commons, 38; North Wind Picture Archives, 56, 58, 72; Public Domain/Harmon Percy Marble/File:MenomineeRes.jpg/Wikimedia Commons, 65; Ullstein Bild via Getty Images, 70; McGhiever/File:Chippewa Lookout.JPG/Wikimedia Commons, 79; AP Photo/Shawano Leader, Donna Hobscheid, 88; AP Photo/Shawano Leader, Cory Dellenbach, 93; cezars/iStockphoto.com, 95; Kutikan/Shutterstock.com, 97; Steven L. Raymer/National Geographic/Getty Images, 100; MPI/Getty Images, 102.

Printed in the United States of America

ACKNOWLEDGMENTS

Several individuals and organizations helped in the research and writing of this book. I would like to especially thank the kind people on the Menominee Reservation in the forests and lakes of Wisconsin who allowed me to make photographs at the Woodland Powwow, also known as the Annual Menominee Nation Contest Powwow, and elsewhere on the reservation.

I am very much indebted to Cavendish Square Publishing for publishing this book. I would like to thank my wife Linda and my children Anna, Sarah, and Luke for their constant inspiration.

CONTENTS

A member of the Menominee Nation waits for the Grand Entry at a powwow in Denver, Colorado, in 2007.

AUTHOR'S NOTE

At the dawn of the twentieth century, Native Americans were thought to be a vanishing race. However, despite four hundred years of warfare, deprivation, and disease, Native Americans have persevered. Countless thousands have lost their lives, but over the course of this century and the last the populations of Native tribes have grown tremendously. Even as America's First People struggle to adapt to modern Western life, they have also kept the flame of their traditions alive—the languages, religions, stories, and the everyday ways of life. An exhilarating renaissance in Native American culture is now sweeping the continent from coast to coast. The First Peoples of North America books depict the social and cultural life of the major nations, from the early history of Native peoples in North America to their present-day struggles for survival and dignity. Historical and contemporary photographs of traditional subjects, as well as period illustrations, are blended throughout each book so that readers may gain a sense of family life in a tipi, a hogan, or a longhouse.

No single book can comprehensively portray the intricate and varied lifeways of an entire tribe, or nation. I only hope that young people will come away with a deeper appreciation for the rich tapestry of Native American culture—both then and now—and a keen desire to learn more about these first Americans.

Cattails (pictured here) were used by the Menominee to make objects such as sleeping mats and baskets.

CHAPTER ONE

We are Wisconsin. We are part of Wisconsin. We've been here 12,000 years.

—Gary Besaw,
Menominee chairman

A CULTURE BEGINS

Thousands of years ago, the first people arrived on North American soil. Most of them crossed the **Bering Strait**, which used to be dry land, creating a walking bridge from between present-day Russia and Alaska. They spread out across the land and established communities, called tribes or nations. Men, women, and children grew up in these communities, forming their own stories, beliefs, and traditions. The Menominee (muh-NOM-uh-nee) were one such group descended from these ancient people. However, their stories of their ancestors varied from other Native tribes.

According to tradition, the Menominee believed that their people originated at the mouth of the Menominee River in northern Wisconsin—just miles east of the location of the present-day Menominee Reservation in Keshena, Wisconsin. Here they lived off the land, fishing, hunting, and gathering resources to eat and to make their clothing and houses. They respected all animals but held the bear—which they considered an ancestor—in especially high regard. The Menominee, like many other tribes, at first had no written language, so they passed their traditions and stories down through word of mouth. One story spoke of their beginnings:

At the mouth of the Menominee River, which flows into Green Bay, the Creator turned a bear named O'wasso into a human being. This great light-colored bear became the first Menominee. However, Bear did not want to be alone. He saw Eagle, who was known as Kine'u, soaring high overhead and called to him, "Eagle, come to me and be my brother." When Eagle descended, he too assumed a human form. Bear and Eagle became "brothers," and they wondered whom else they might ask to join them—just as Beaver approached them.

A bald eagle snatches fish from a lake in Wisconsin.

Beaver, called Namalkukiu, asked to join them, and was adopted as their younger brother. Soon afterward, as Bear and Eagle stood on the banks of the river, they saw Sturgeon, or Noma'eu. Bear adopted Sturgeon as a younger brother who would become keeper of the wild rice. Then the Elk, known as Omas'kos, was adopted as a younger brother and water carrier. In this same manner, Wolf, Moose, Crane, and other animals were also adopted as brothers. They each came to represent one of the **clans** of the tribe. And this is how the Menominee came to be.

The Menominee Begin

The Menominee once inhabited a vast territory, more than 10 million acres (4,046,856 hectares) of land in what is now Wisconsin and the Upper Peninsula of Michigan. The Menominee themselves trace their descent back at least as far as the Ice Age of thirteen thousand years ago when the Great Lakes region was covered by an immense sheet of ice known as a glacier. Hundreds of feet thick, the glacier leveled hills and carved out lakes as it moved southward.

However, not all of the land was covered by ice, and early people lived there, hunting mammoths and other large beasts near Lake Michigan in southern Wisconsin. Forests of spruce and fir, along with birch, oak, ash, linden, and cedar, blanketed the southern regions untouched by the glacier. As the glacier melted, it left rivers that flowed southward, including the Wolf, Peshtigo, and Wisconsin Rivers. As the climate became warmer and drier, these trees, grasses, and other plants gradually spread northward. Then animals, including mammoths, giant beavers, barren ground caribou, elk, and deer, which thrived in a cold and moist climate, also moved northward. They were followed, finally, by humans—the ancestors of the Menominee people.

According to some archaeologists, the Menominee may have descended from the Mound Builders of approximately a thousand years ago. There are ancient mounds on the present-day reservation. However, according to **oral tradition**, the Menominee fought the Mound Builders and drove them from the region. Menominee stories also do not indicate any relationship

For centuries, the Menominee have made their homes in forests.

with the Mound Builders. However, they do tell stories of different tribes: the Bear clan and the Eagle clan, for instance. Stories depict the Bear and Eagle becoming brothers. In Menominee tradition, many different tribes, including the Bear and Eagle clans, came together to form what is known as the Menominee Nation today.

The Menominee ranged from the Upper Peninsula of Michigan south to Illinois and west to Minnesota. They referred to themselves as either Kiash Matchitiwuk, which means "the Ancient Ones," or Omenomenew, or Omanomineu, pronounced "O-man-o-me-na-oo," but the meaning of the term is unclear. For countless centuries they gathered wild rice, hunted whitetail

This painting shows Jean Nicolet arriving in Green Bay, Wisconsin.

deer, and speared the large sturgeon migrating up the streams, until their religious leaders, known as Dreamers, told them that men would soon arrive from the east. It is believed that Menominee Dreamers prophesied the arrival of light-skinned people in large boats at La Baye (now called Green Bay). In 1634, this prophecy came true when the French explorer Jean Nicolet entered the bay in search of a route to the East. It is estimated that there were about three thousand to four thousand Menominee people at that time. Not long after Nicolet's arrival, the Menominee became involved in a fur trade with the French, and these proud, independent people soon came to rely on trade goods as they adopted a new way of life.

Becoming the Menominee

When the Bear clan and Eagle clan got together to form the Menominee tribe, they were helped by a spiritual hero named **Manabush**. To the leader of the Bear clan Manabush said, "I give these things to you, and you shall always have them—the river, the fish, the wild rice, and the sugar trees."

The Menominee traded animal furs with the French.

Birch bark was used to build Menominee houses and canoes.

For as long as anyone can remember, the Menominee people have lived among the forests, lakes, and rivers around Lake Michigan. The climate was marked by mild summers and bitterly cold, snowy winters.

Over time, Menominee territory came to include the lands on northeastern Wisconsin lying west of Lake Michigan and Green Bay, with the northern boundary reaching into northeastern Michigan and west to the

Mississippi River. This land was mostly flat and heavily forested. There were occasional sandy patches and rolling plains to the south. The rivers and streams formed a water network for travel among the many lakes of northern Michigan and Wisconsin that joined Lake Michigan.

Conifer and mixed hardwood forests blanketed most of Menominee territory. Maple, elm, oak, hickory, chestnut, and beech trees reached northward, blending with stands of white birch trees and the coniferous forests of white pine, jack pine, and white spruce. Scattered among the evergreens were poplar and aspen trees, while tamarack, black spruce, and white cedar grew in the marshes of the northern forests. On the forest floor, people gathered nuts, berries, herbs, and roots. They used roots and plants not only as food but also in religious rites and as medicines.

Northern Wisconsin and Michigan also abounded in wildlife, such as bears, deer, wolves, coyotes, foxes, wolverines, and lynxes. There were also beavers, otters, muskrats, porcupines, raccoons, woodchucks, rabbits, weasels, and minks, all of which the Menominee hunted or trapped. The streams and lakes also teemed with fish and fowl, especially ducks and geese in flocks so large they often blackened the skies. The Menominee hunted deer for their meat and hides, but they favored the greasy flesh of the bear. They traditionally caught many kinds of fur-bearing animals, but over time they came to concentrate on trapping beavers, whose valuable pelts were eagerly sought by the French in what became an international trade.

The Menominee paddled their swift canoes throughout their territory. Along the riverbanks they traded wild rice, corn, or animal pelts with their friends—notably the French—and made war against their enemies. They hunted and gathered in the woods and fields. Yet over time, they came to rely on crops of corn, beans, and squash, especially when the wild rice crop failed or game was scarce. Although trees had to be cleared to build dwellings called **wigwams** near the rivers, the land was fertile and easily worked with stone tools.

Like other Native people, the Menominee lived according to the cycle of the seasons. In the spring, the sap flowed and the buds emerged on the trees. They **tapped** maple trees and boiled down the sap to make sugar. When the soil thawed and was warmed by the sun, they planted their crops. In early summer, they gathered wild berries before the long, dry months of July and August when the ears of corn ripened on the clumps of cornstalks in their fields.

Come autumn, the leaves of the trees briefly turned brilliant red, yellow, and orange. Corn leaves and stalks faded to tan, pumpkins glowed orange against the dark earth, and drying beans rattled in their shells. The women harvested these crops and then the Menominee paddled canoes along the marshy edges of rivers to gather wild rice before the first cold winds swept down upon them. Through the long winter, the snows blanketed the land. Frozen over, the rivers and lakes disappeared under the drifts, and people settled around the fires in their wigwams, trudging only short distances in their snowshoes in search of a rabbit or deer. However, game was scarce and hard to hunt in the winter, so they relied on their stores of wild rice, dried meat, and corn.

For generations, the Menominee sustained themselves by living off what resources the land, forests, and fields provided. Their communities flourished and their traditions were passed down from generation to generation. This was their home and the home of their ancestors. It was hoped that it would always be a place they could dwell and grow in for decades to come.

The landscape of
Marinette, Wisconsin

Menominee comes from the Algonquian word maṇomin *meaning "wild rice."*

BUILDING A CIVILIZATION

When the Menominee came to Wisconsin and the Lake Michigan area, they established communities. Men, women, and children banded together to form villages. Over time, these villages became thriving civilizations with their own identity, language, and beliefs.

Starting Out

Before the arrival of the French and the fur trade, the Menominee came together in small villages along the Menominee River during the spring, summer, and fall. Known as Menekaunee, their

This map shows Native American boundaries in 1825 according to the Treaty of Prairie du Chien.

principal village was situated near present-day Marinette, Wisconsin. Because they often had to travel in search of food, they also set up outlying camps for gathering and hunting. From their main villages, they journeyed up to 100 miles (160 kilometers) through northern Wisconsin and into Michigan's Upper Peninsula. During the winter, as the snows deepened, they dispersed into small bands and moved into camps in the forests. They hunted for game and lived off of stores of food gathered or grown during the warmer months.

In the summer village, they also built sweat lodges, huts in which the women secluded themselves during childbirth and at other times, places for dreaming and **fasting**, and the lodge of the religious leader, or shaman.

Housing

The Menominee lived in rectangular, peaked-roofed lodges called longhouses in their summer villages. They made the framework for these houses with peeled logs, which were covered with sheets of bark. Inside, the dwelling had plenty of space and remained fairly cool throughout the summer. Each lodge had a central fire pit with a smoke hole in the roof overhead. This hole had a bark flap to control the amount of air that drew the smoke out of the lodge. At one time, several Menominee families lived in the largest of these longhouses, with partitions made of reeds and raised platforms for sleeping. However, in later years, the longhouse served only as a gathering place for religious ceremonies.

In their winter camps, the Menominee took shelter in circular-shaped wigwams with domed roofs. To build one of these huts, they formed the arched frame by bending saplings to a center point and lashing them together. They covered the frame with sheets of elm, cedar, or **birch bark**. Sometimes, they sheathed the dwelling with mats woven from cattail reeds instead of bark. The wigwam had a single, low door and a smoke hole in the top of the roof. A fire for heat and cooking was kept burning in a small pit in the middle of the floor. The Menominee also lined the inside of the

Menominee families built wigwams in which they lived.

wigwam with cattail mats to provide better insulation. Women wove reeds gathered from the lakeshore into rugs for the floor. Here, the Menominee met for meals, told stories, and worked on handicrafts through the long northern winters.

Government

Menominee society was organized around a complex structure of clans, which were named for various animals, so that each clan had its own special symbol, or **totem**. Clan membership influenced all social relationships, including government, marriage, and family life. Clan members were considered related, and individuals could not marry a person of the same clan. Upon marriage, a couple usually went to live with the husband's family.

Menominee member James Frechette Jr. used only traditional tools to carve this bear from a tree.

Originally, there were three Menominee divisions. As the population grew, two more were added. The five main divisions were the Bear, the Thunderers (represented by the Golden Eagle), the Crane, the Wolf, and the Moose. Each division, or **phratry**, consisted of a principal clan and several other member clans. When treaties were first being made with the United States government, the Menominee system was composed of thirty-four clans grouped into five phratries, as follows:

Owas'sse we'dishi'anun Bear phratry

Owa'sse	Bear (principal clan)
Kita'mi	Porcupine
Miqka'no	Turtle
Mikek'	Otter

Noma'eu	Sturgeon
Naku'ti	Sunfish
O'sass	Muskrat

Ina'maqki'u wi'dishi'anun Thunderer phratry

Kine'u	Golden Eagle (principal clan)
Piwat'inot	Beaver (former name Noma'i)
Shawan'nani	Fork-tail Hawk
Pinash'iu	Bald Eagle
Pakesh'tsheke'u	Swift-flying Hawk
Pe'kike'kune	Winter Hawk
Ke'shewa'toshe	Sparrow Hawk
Maq'kwoka'ni	Red-tail Hawk
Kaka'ke	Crow
Inaq'tek	Raven
	Fish Hawk

Moqwai'o wi'dishi'anun Wolf phratry

Moqwai'o	Wolf (principal clan)
Anam'	Dog
Apaehsos	White Tail Deer
Wakoh	Fox
	Pine Squirrel

Ota'tshia wi'dishi'anun Crane phratry

Ota'tshia	Crane (principal clan)
Shakshak'eu	Great Heron

Os'se	"Old Woman" Duck
O'kawa'siku	Coot
	Loon
	Turkey Buzzard

Mo's wi'dishi'anun	**Moose phratry**
Mo's	Moose (principal clan)
Oma'skos	Elk
Waba'shiu	Marten
Wu'tshik	Fisher
	Racoon

In this system, each phratry was considered an excellent source of knowledge in certain fields. The members of the Bear phratry were expert speakers and keepers of the law. Those in the Thunderers phratry valued freedom and justice. The Moose phratry emphasized community as well as individual security. The members of the Crane phratry were skilled in architecture, construction, and art. Members of the Wolf phratry specialized in hunting and gathering.

Each family had a hereditary chief. This chief served on a village council with other chiefs. The chief of the Bear phratry also served as the head chief of the council. Members of the council managed general matters in the community and were special leaders in war and religious affairs. The Menominee also had war chiefs who gained prominence through skill and courage in battle. They acted as keepers of the tribal war medicine, spokesmen for the hereditary leaders, directors of public celebrations, and guardians of the

This Beaver Woman carving by James Frechette Jr. commemorates the only female Menominee clan.

wild rice at harvest time. Regarded as speakers of the tribe, these leaders drew their power from the tribal members. Acting as a whole, tribal members reached decisions through consensus, then empowered the leaders to take action.

Alliances and Enemies

While the Menominee lived close to other Native tribes, such as the Fox, they lived separately from them, except to trade. Other Native groups called the Menominee "Menomini," after the **Algonquian** word *manomin* meaning "wild rice," which was an important crop grown by the Menominee. Over the centuries, the name has remained.

The Menominee made alliances within their own clans and worked together. Over time, however, other Native tribes sought to take their land and their livelihood. In the late 1600s, Menominee tribes living in Michigan fled to Wisconsin. They were worried the Iroquois, a strong band of Native Americans, would take control of Menominee and other Native

The Iroquois were a strong Native American group that caused problems for the Menominee and other Native tribes.

lands nearby. The Menominee living in Wisconsin quickly took in their tribesmen and women, becoming an even larger entity.

Europeans arrived in the seventeenth century, first with Jean Nicolet and then with other French traders. Their arrival signaled a new era for the Menominee people. Never before had the Menominee encountered richly dressed men or their strange ways. They embarked on peaceful negotiations, trading with them and learning from them. At first, these alliances proved beneficial. However, over the years, the Menominee way of life slowly changed.

A Menominee couple stands near cornstalks in their garden on the Menominee Indian Reservation in Wisconsin.

*The Menominee
worked hard to
create and sustain
their civilization.*

LIFE IN THE MENOMINEE NATION

L ife for the early Menominee consisted of many tasks to ensure survival. They hunted and gathered and traded with other tribes when needed. Later, they would welcome the Europeans and learn from them. Throughout the centuries, the Menominee developed a thriving culture with many ceremonies, celebrations, and rituals that defined them as a group.

The Life Cycle

The Menominee lived in harmony not only with animals and plants but also with the earth itself, as well as with the sun, the moon, and the stars. Their lives revolved around the daily tasks of raising children and preparing meals, and the seasonal activities of hunting, farming, and the harvesting of wild rice. Through these practices, everyone in the family, clan, and band learned the lessons of life. It is how the people came to understand the mystery of birth, the complexity of youth, and the acceptance of old age and death.

Being Born

When a woman was about to give birth, she moved into a small hut away from the village. There she had her baby, who was promptly bathed and placed on an ornately carved **cradleboard** decorated with beadwork and hung with toys and charms. Holes were made in its moccasins to prevent any evil spirit from encouraging the newborn to leave its parents and return to the spirit world. The infant would have to refuse because its moccasins were too worn to undertake so long a journey. The child was then given a personal name, often by a shaman. Later in life, children received a new name in honor of some courageous deed.

For two or three years, until it was able to walk, the baby remained swaddled in bulrush down in the cradleboard for most of the time. The mother carried the cradleboard on her back or stood it against the lodge so that the baby could watch her as she worked at the cooking fire.

A Menominee mother carries her child in a cradleboard.

Growing Up

As they grew up, children were taught to respect the elderly and the natural world. According to a saying, they learned to "Never speak ill of anything you see, it may be a **manitou** [a spirit]." From the age of six, boys underwent rigorous training that began with a morning plunge in often icy water. Parents emphasized practical training for their children. Fathers were largely responsible for teaching their sons. Boys became skilled with the bow and arrow in hunting and warfare, as well as making and paddling canoes, fishing for sturgeons, and many other tasks in the woods and water. Girls were very close to their mothers, learning how to take care of the household, gather wild rice, work in the cornfields, and make clothing. Children also learned the beliefs and customs of their people. From an early age, both girls and boys were encouraged to fast, so that they would someday be able to endure the long, difficult rituals of puberty.

When a girl had her first period, she had to move into a small lodge away from the community for ten days. She used special utensils that could not be touched by others. Thereafter, she had to retire to this hut every month when she menstruated.

When they came of age, both girls and boys moved away from the village into a small hut, just big enough for one person, and went on a vision quest or dream fast for eight to ten days. They blackened their faces, as in mourning, and could not touch a drop of water or a morsel of food. They prayed for a vision that would guide them in the future. They did not see or speak to anyone. If they had not had a dream after eight days, the parents came to them and offered a bowl of charcoal and a bowl of food. If the faster chose the food, he or she would give up and try a dream fast again at another time. If the charcoal was chosen, the faster smeared it on his or her face, and continued the ordeal. After they had completed their dream fast and learned the skills needed to be an adult, young people were considered ready to be married.

Marrying

A young man sometimes courted at night, visiting the lodge of the young woman he loved. However, parents usually chose wives for their sons, following customs given to their ancestors by Manabush. If a young man proved acceptable to the parents of a young woman, his relatives presented suitable clothing for the bride and gifts of wild rice, maple sugar, mats, and other goods to her parents. Parents of both the bride and groom advised them on their duties as husband and wife. The groom's parents then hosted a great feast for the bride's family. The parents again counseled the newlyweds, and the bride then went to live in the young man's lodge. At the end of the year, her parents offered gifts to his parents. These gifts had to be at least equal in value to those which they had previously received. Everyone hoped for a long, happy marriage. However, if the couple did not get along, they could divorce each other if both agreed to the separation.

Dying

When a person died, the body was dressed in the finest clothing and ornaments, and the face was painted. Mourners gathered for two days and two nights, blackening their faces and putting on old clothes. In the evenings, selected people entered the lodge and sang death songs to the rhythm of gourd rattles. The next day the body was dressed in its second-best clothes and laid out with tobacco and other gifts placed near the head. The body was carried through a hole at the back of the lodge to confuse any evil spirit that might want to follow the funeral procession. The mourners then proceeded to the cemetery, where the body was laid out and a feast of the dead was held. There was a ceremonial smoke after which the body was placed beside the grave. Traditionally, food, utensils, and weapons were buried with the deceased to help the soul in its journey to the spirit world. A bundle of new clothes along with a lock of the deceased's hair in the center was presented at the funeral and taken home. After the burial, mourners returned home in a roundabout way so that no ghosts could follow them.

Warring

Although generally a peaceful tribe, the Menominee were able and willing to defend their territory when necessary. At times, they also invaded enemy territory and attacked other tribes. They were friendly with the Winnebago, and most often fought the Sauk and Fox. In the early 1700s, the Menominee sided with the French, who had taken control of the Wisconsin area, in what became known as the Fox Wars. The Fox tribe had tried to remove the French from their land. Being allied to the French for their fur trading, the Menominee protected them.

Warriors sometimes raided Osage camps and allied with the Santee Sioux to venture up the Mississippi

A Menominee warrior, Amiskquew

River to attack Mandan villages in North Dakota. They again sided with the French during the French and Indian War, and later joined the cause of the British in the American Revolution. Later, during the Black Hawk War in 1832, the Menominee helped American troops to

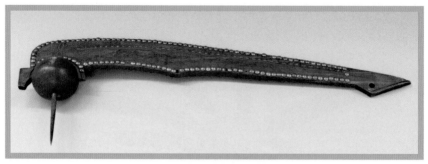

This war club from the early nineteenth century has a large spike coming from it. Menominee warriors used the club to hurt and kill their enemies.

defeat the Sauk and Fox and force these tribes to move west of the Mississippi River.

When going into battle, the Menominee relied on sacred war bundles for strength, courage, and good fortune. It was believed that the Thunderers had given the first war bundle to their people. Thereafter, war bundles were given to selected men and women through dreams. The small, oval-shaped pouches held amulets, or sacred objects, that gave exceptional powers to warriors. These included roots that were said to make warriors invisible, snakeskins meant to allow a stealthy approach, and the skin of a swallow that was thought to make the warrior as elusive as this small bird in flight. A tiny war club was believed to have the power of thunder. Twice a year, in the spring and fall, the Menominee gathered for a feast and dance, where they offered sacrifices to the war bundle and honored the bundle owners.

When the Menominee declared a war, runners were sent to each of their villages. Bearing tobacco and a string of **wampum**, the runners were painted red so the bundle owners would immediately know that it was time to gather their warriors. The bundle owner then

The People and Culture of the Menominee

led his warriors away from the village to a secluded place in the forest. Here, the warriors made a lodge of tree branches, where the war bundles were opened and sacrifices were made, followed by a war dance.

Bearing the war bundles, the war party then set forth. When they arrived near the enemy's camp, the owner again opened the war bundle and sang to the rhythm of a deer-hoof rattle. He then gave one of the sacred objects from the war bundle to each of the warriors.

Carrying bows, arrows, knives, and war clubs, usually the warriors attacked just before dawn. The Menominee wielded two styles of war clubs, each about 2 feet (0.6 meters) in length. One was ball headed, sometimes with a deadly spike in the knob, and the other was angled like a dog's hind leg and set with a stone blade. Warriors were also armed with knives and bows and arrows. They made long, simple bows of hickory, ash, or other wood that was both strong and supple. The shaft was shaped with a curved knife and dressed with bear grease. The Menominee crafted arrows from hard, straight-grained wood. They attached split turkey or hawk feathers to the wooden shafts and tipped them with arrowheads, or points, of chipped flint or quartz, antler tips, turtle claws, and occasionally copper. Turtle claw and copper arrowheads were used only for warfare. The Menominee thought that turtle claw points struck the enemy with the magical power of the turtle.

The warriors took scalps and the first to kill an enemy was given a wampum belt. After the battle, the warriors returned to their village, where a victory dance was held. The warriors then danced with the scalps strung on a pole as a relative—preferably a sister—

came forward and ritually washed the "blood from their hands." She then took the scalps, which became her trophies. If the warrior had no female relatives, his scalps were kept in the war bundle until the next feast. Then they were given to other warriors and their sisters.

Tending the Land

For many centuries, the Menominee tapped the maple trees in their homeland, as Manabush had taught them. In late February and March, families moved to the sugar camps, where they lived for several weeks. Working together, they drove wooden chips into the trunk and made a gash in the bark, just above the chip. Maple sap dripped into a birch bark pouch hung just beneath the gash. When the pouch was full, people emptied it into a large bark trough. Here, they boiled the sap by placing hot rocks in the container—day and night until it thickened into maple syrup. The syrup was poured into another trough and stirred with wooden paddles.

After the Menominee encountered French traders, they acquired iron kettles, which could be placed directly over the fire. This made it easier to convert maple syrup into sugar. Some of the sugar might be traded for European goods—blankets, rifles, or household utensils. The rest was placed in birch bark pouches and stored away for later use. Over the course of the year, the maple sugar was eaten as a food, along with wild rice, fish, deer, and other meat. It was also used to flavor vegetables and to sweeten soups and stews.

After the maple sugaring, the Menominee fished for sturgeons during the **spawning** runs. Then they returned to their villages along the rivers where the women picked wild berries and planted cornfields. Through the summer and autumn, they gathered wild blueberries, gooseberries, blackberries, raspberries, cherries, chokecherries, grapes, and cranberries. They also harvested the seeds, roots, and leaves of wild plants, such as wild potatoes, wild onions, and milkweed. In the autumn, they collected acorns from pin oaks and white oaks, and hickory nuts, hazelnuts, beechnuts, and butternuts that had fallen with the leaves.

Women also planted small gardens near their summer homes. They first broke the soil with short wooden hoes and planted corn in hills. The Menominee grew two kinds of corn—early blue corn and a white corn that ripened later. They also grew popcorn, which the Menominee sometimes called mouse corn. Women boiled and roasted ears of fresh corn, like sweet corn. When the corn had fully ripened, women also ground the hard kernels into a coarse meal, which could be stored and used when needed through the winter. Cornmeal was added to a wide variety of dishes.

The summer was short, so people could grow only enough corn, beans, and squash to supplement their stocks of game, fish, wild rice, and other gathered foods. However, since corn, beans, and squash could be dried and stored, these crops were a vital source of food during the long winters when game was scarce.

Wild rice was one of the most important foods of the Menominee. Only distantly related to rice, this grass sprouted every spring in the shallow waters of marshes, lakes, and streams in the north. Wild rice grew through the summer until it was ready to harvest in the early autumn. In the morning, the Menominee set out in their canoes. While a man stood in the stern and pushed through the thick grass with a pole, a woman sat in the prow. With a cedar stick about 3 feet (0.9 m) long, she bent clumps of wild rice stalks over the upper edge of the canoe's sides. With a shorter stick, she gently knocked the ripe seeds of rice into the bottom of the canoe. The wild rice that dropped into the water became the seeds for next year's crop. When the canoe was filled, the couple went back to shore and took their harvest to camp. That evening, people held a feast of thanks at which they ate a little of the wild rice.

After picking out bits of stalks, small stones, or twigs, women spread the wild rice on blankets or sheets of birch bark to dry in the sun. In later years, the Menominee parched, or heated, several pounds of the grains in iron kettles acquired from European traders and placed over hot coals. With wooden paddles, they continually stirred the wild rice so that the grains would not be scorched. Parching darkened the grains and gave a smoky flavor to the wild rice. It also loosened the outer husks, which were removed by "dancing the rice." The parched grains were poured into a large shallow wooden bowl sunk in the ground or a hole lined with deerskin. Putting on soft, clean, high-cuff moccasins, a man danced lightly on the wild rice. Occasionally, he tapped the wild rice with a threshing stick.

The final step was to winnow, or separate, the grain from the loosened hulls, or chaff. On a windy afternoon, women poured the wild rice into birch bark trays and tossed it into the air. The autumn breeze carried away the light hulls, while the heavy grains fell back into

RECIPE

WILD RICE AND VENISON STEW

The following recipe combines two traditional Menominee foods.

INGREDIENTS

3.5 pounds (1.6 kilograms) venison (or beef)

1 cup (237 milliliters) flour

3 tablespoons (44 mL) bacon grease

2 quarts (1.9 liters) water

2 onions, peeled and quartered

1.5 cups (355 mL) wild rice, rinsed

1 teaspoon (5 mL) mixed thyme, basil, and marjoram

1 teaspoon (5 mL) dried parsley

1 teaspoon (5 mL) salt

¼ teaspoon (1.2 mL) ground pepper

Cut meat into 1-inch (2.54 cm) cubes and roll in flour. Brown the cubes in bacon grease in a large pot. Add 2 quarts (1.9 L) of water, herbs, onions, salt, and pepper. Cover pot and bring to a boil. Lower heat and simmer for about two hours or until meat is tender. Add more water if needed.

Add wild rice. Cover and simmer for about twenty minutes. Stir and simmer uncovered for an additional twenty minutes, or until rice is tender. Serves six to eight people.

the tray. Wild rice was stored in skin bags or birch bark containers. It was boiled in water and eaten with berries, and often added to many soups and stews. People stayed in the wild rice fields for several weeks, harvesting through the day, and drumming and dancing at night. It was a good time to visit with friends and family. At the end of the harvest, families celebrated with a festival of thanksgiving.

Catching Food

The Menominee depended on hunting and trapping for much of their food, as well as for furs and skins for their clothing. They hunted large game, such as moose and bear, but deer was their most important source of meat and hides. With bow and arrow, lone hunters stalked deer, caught them in snares, or waited for them to approach salt licks or drinking places. They also called deer by imitating the bleat of a newborn fawn. However, this call could be dangerous, since it not only attracted does but also wolves and wildcats. Groups of men also used dogs to chase deer past hunters hidden in the bushes. Most often, however, men cut down brush to make a V-shaped trap that narrowed to an opening at the bottom. Beating the bushes, they drove the deer into the wide opening of this trap. Hunters waited to shoot the deer as they tried to escape through the opening.

The Menominee hunted and trapped bears only after a sacred ritual. In early times, armed with spears and stone, hunters stalked bears and killed them single-handedly, often at close range. Men also trapped bears in **deadfalls** made of heavy logs weighted with stones.

Propped up with a pole and baited with honey or beaver musk—and later apples or pork—the log dropped just as the bear yanked at the bait. The Menominee also caught bears in large snares and pitfalls dug and covered over on their paths. After they came into contact with the French, the Menominee traded for large steel traps that caught the bear by the leg. This trap was chained to a log that the bear dragged through the woods. It was easily pursued and killed.

Men also hunted or trapped other game, including rabbits, muskrats, minks, otters, beavers, raccoons, martens, foxes, wolves, and lynxes, for their meat and fur. Rabbits were most often snared by simple nooses set across their paths. Other animals were caught in deadfalls or nets woven from nettle fibers and basswood twine. Men also hunted birds, including ruffed grouse, ducks, and geese.

The Menominee depended on fish for much of their food. They fished all year long with nets, spears, hooks, lines, and traps. On large lakes, they dragged long nets made of bark cords and nettle-stalk twine, with which they caught great numbers of fish. They also speared fish through holes in the ice during the winter. One fisherman jiggled a lure in the ice hole, while the other stood ready to thrust the spear into any fish that approached. In the summer, they spearfished from birch bark canoes at night. One man held a flaming torch whose light attracted fish while the other was poised to spear them. The Menominee also tied a string onto a hook made of bone, wood, or copper. They lowered the baited hook and line into the water, often trolling, or pulling, behind a canoe, wriggling the line to attract fish. The Menominee wove twigs and branches into traps to catch both small and large fish. Huge sturgeons were often caught with a fish **weir**, or trap, which was a V-shaped row of rocks set across a stream. The fish were guided to the narrow opening where men waited to club them.

The fish were cooked fresh—either boiled or roasted on spits. They were also hung on scaffolds and dried in the sun, or smoked over a fire. Large fish were split and drawn (inner organs cleaned out), then grilled, dried, or smoked. Small fish were smoked and pounded into a coarse meal, then cooked with cornmeal mush, wild rice, and other dishes. Highly prized, sturgeon eggs were eaten fresh or dried for later use.

Birds were usually stewed in a pot with wild rice and other ingredients, while meat from deer and other animals was usually boiled or roasted. Meat was also sliced into thin strips and dried for later use. Melted fat, or tallow, was stored in the bladder or large intestine of an animal. It was used to flavor berries, wild rice, and many other dishes. Considered a delicacy, marrow was scooped out of the bones with a willow stick. Animal bones were also pounded into a powder and mixed with dried meat and tallow for a high-energy food.

The Menominee usually had two meals a day, but a pot was always left simmering over the fire. Chunks of meat were picked out of the pots with the fingers or sticks. Using bark as dishes, people ate either with their fingers or spoons made of wood, clamshells, or birch bark.

Clothes and Accessories

Women worked hard to tan deerskins to make **buckskin**, which they sometimes bleached snowy white. They cut the buckskin into pieces, which they skillfully sewed into clothing for their families.

Traditionally, women wore only a buckskin skirt wrapped around their waists and occasionally a poncho-style buckskin shawl for warmth. Later, they adopted a buckskin dress with straps and sleeves, under which they wore a skirt woven with nettle fibers. Men wore tanned leather **breechcloths** with flaps that hung down, front and back, to mid-thigh. As the weather cooled, they wore simply cut buckskin shirts and added buckskin leggings.

Women decorated buckskin clothing with shell beads and dyed porcupine quills. In quilling, which was one of their oldest handicrafts, women first softened the quills in water, then flattened them with an antler or bone tool. The quills were then dyed, and short pieces were carefully sewn onto clothing, as well as medicine bags and bark boxes. Traditionally, the Menominee favored geometric designs, but since about 1830, they came to prefer elaborate floral and realistic patterns in much of their work. Early in the twentieth century, they learned a technique called ribbon appliqué. Since then, they have used strips to decorate skirts, shawls, shirts, leggings, and breechcloths, which have evolved into an apron style with lavish decoration.

Both men and women also wore soft-soled moccasins made of a single piece of leather with a

This pair of moccasins from 1910 are an example of Menominee craftsmanship.

The People and Culture of the Menominee

seam at the toe and wide flaps. Some moccasins had high cuffs that were turned up and tied around the ankle when threshing wild rice. Snowshoes were essential when men went hunting in the winter. They were made of ash, steamed and bent into a rounded shape and tied at the back in a style called "catfish." Craftsmen added crossbars to strengthen the frame, which was woven with rawhide thongs in a hexagonal pattern. Leather straps held the toes and heels in place as the hunter trudged through the snow.

Women also made buckskin into lightweight robes. However, during the winter, people needed to wrap themselves in thick, heavy robes. The Menominee traded with tribes to the west for buffalo robes, which were painted on the skin side in the Plains style. Women also made bear skins into heavy robes, but the small pelts of beaver made the warmest robes. They cut rabbit skins into long spiral strips, which they wove into robes that were very warm, but fragile.

Menominee men and women both wore fur hoods in the winter. Women traditionally wore their hair loose or in two braids pulled tightly to the back of their heads. Men often favored otter fur hats in a turban style. These hats were worn with the otter tail at the side or back. Some men liked to wear headdresses with feathers sticking out at random. Others simply wore their hair long, with one or two feathers attached. Still others favored a roach, or Mohawk, made of a turkey beard. Many simply shaved their heads leaving a scalplock, or ponytail, which either fell from the crown or was wrapped on top of the head and tied with a feather or two.

Women crafted rectangular pouches and shoulder bags for themselves. These were made of dyed plant fibers, shredded bark, and buffalo hair adorned with **quillwork** and moose-hair embroidery. The designs often featured Thunderers and other sacred beings, along with figures of people and animals. Women also skillfully finger-wove nettle, shredded basswood bark, and buffalo hair into sashes with long fringes on the ends. They wore the sashes around their waists or wound like turbans on their heads. Men often carried a knife in a finely crafted sheath hung around their necks.

The Menominee liked to wear many strings of necklaces made of chunks of copper or shells. They especially favored hair pipe beads, which were shaped like long white tubes. Both men and women pierced their ears and dangled ornaments from each small hole. Strings of hair pipe beads were also hung from the brow on either side of the face.

The Menominee painted their faces and occasionally their bodies. It is not believed that they tattooed themselves. Men often painted two parallel black bars across the face, red designs on the cheeks, or one part of the face black. Women usually painted a round red spot on each cheek.

As the Menominee began to trade with the French, they quickly replaced buckskin with cloth when making garments. They came to use glass beads instead of porcupine quills and beads. Blankets replaced buffalo robes, but women continued their exceptional weaving, and shoulder bags were widely traded. They came to be called friendship bags because they were often given to friends.

Arts and Crafts

The Menominee made nearly all the household items, tools, and weapons that they needed for survival. Along with making clothing and accessories, women wove many kinds of mats from rushes, cattails, and cedar bark. Mats were used to cover buildings, including large mats 3 feet (0.9 m) wide and 6 to 12 feet (1.8 to 3.7 m) long for the medicine lodge. Women cut green reeds from the lakeshore, which they steeped in boiling water and bleached in the sun. Then they dyed the reeds with pigments from blueberries, blackberries, wild plums, chokecherries, lamb's-quarters, butternut roots, the inner bark of sumac, and other plants to obtain beautiful colors. The leaves were then woven with thread made from basswood fibers. To make bark mats, they stripped the inner bark of cedar trees, which was then cut into strips about 1 inch (2.54 cm) wide. Some mats were nearly white, but others were dyed dark red or black. By weaving different colors, women created striking diamond or zigzag patterns.

Baskets were woven in the same manner as bark mats. Women made strips, or splits, by hammering black elm limbs with a wooden mallet until the fibers could be separated. The strips were coiled up until ready to be woven. Then they were soaked in water. The flexible strips were woven into useful baskets of various shapes and styles. The Menominee also twisted the inner bark of basswood to make string and twine.

To make pottery, women carefully selected clay, which was mixed with powdered shells of freshwater

This box, made of birch, was decorated with porcupine quills. It was made by members of the Menominee tribe.

The People and Culture of the Menominee

clams. The shell powder tempered, or strengthened, the clay. Water was added, and the clay was kneaded into a stiff paste. The clay was then smeared over a ball of twine, smoothed with a stick, and dried in the sun. The end of the twine was left sticking out of the pot opening so that the ball could be unraveled, leaving a hard clay pot. More clay was smeared on the inside of the pot. The outside was coated with fine clay and designs were applied with a sharp stick. Two holes were then drilled at the top edge for handles made of basswood twine. The pot was then dried again.

Men made tools, household items, and weapons, including knives, war clubs, and bows and arrows. They carved lovely wooden bowls, ladles, and spoons. They fashioned bone awls and needles. However, they were especially skilled at making canoes—both dugouts and birch bark canoes. They made dugouts from a single trunk, preferably from a butternut tree. They believed that this heavy wood better resisted decay than other available woods. They painstakingly hollowed out the log by alternately burning with a row of small fires and chopping out wood with stone axes. About 20 feet (6 m) long, the canoe was then expertly scraped inside and out so that it was gracefully shaped with sides just 1 to 1.5 inches (2.54 to 3.81 cm) thick.

In crafting birch bark canoes, the Menominee lashed together a frame from white cedar, which was light, flexible, and sturdy. To make ribs for the frame, they thinned pieces of wood with a drawing knife then shaped them to fit the curved shape of the canoe. The ribs were tied to the gunwales and strengthened with crosspieces. Large sheets of birch bark were stitched

The People and Culture of the Menominee

together, laid out on the ground, and the framework was placed on them. The bark was drawn up, and posts were driven into the ground to temporarily hold it in place. The covering was then stitched along the gunwales and the bottom was lined with thin wooden slats to protect the delicate birch bark. Finally, the men sealed the seams and any small holes or knotholes with pine resin.

They carved paddles from cedar or other light wood. Birch bark canoe paddles were about 4 feet (1.2 m) long, half of which was the blade, which was 4 to 6 inches (10.1 to 15.2 cm) wide. In their finished canoes, the Menominee paddled great distances along the rivers and across the lakes of the north country.

The Menominee worked hard to create and sustain their civilization. Eventually, however, they adopted European ways and became reliant on goods from that area to maintain their altered lifestyle.

The Menominee had deeply rooted traditions, including ways of treating the sick with a medicine man called a shaman.

*From oral traditions,
we manage to keep
our creation story.*

—*Through Tribal Eyes*,
documentary by
the College of
Menominee Nation

BELIEFS OF THE MENOMINEE

The Menominee had many beliefs and religious or spiritual practices. Each belief was important to the tribe and celebrated with reverence and respect. Although some of these traditions are no longer practiced, a few remain upheld by the Menominee Nation today.

Religion

The Menominee believed that the earth was an island between an upper and a lower world.

This illustration shows what it was like inside a longhouse.

The upper world represented good and the lower world evil. The upper and lower worlds also had other layers. Known as **Mecawetok**, the sun was the Creator, or Great Spirit, at the highest level, followed by the Thunderers, or Thunderbirds, and the Morning Star. Then there were the Golden Eagle, which symbolized war, and the other birds, led by the Bald Eagle. In the lower world, the Horned Serpent inhabited the level just below the earth. The Horned Serpent prowled the lakes and streams, where he tried to capsize boats and carry people down to the underworld. The White Deer, from whom the Medicine Dance was thought to have originated, lived in the next level, followed by the level of the Underwater Panther. The Great White Bear, from whom the Menominee were said to have descended, lived in the lowest level. Traditionally, the Menominee

The People and Culture of the Menominee

believed that other spirits, known as manitous, inhabited the earth.

Individuals sought to obtain supernatural power with the help of a guardian spirit who was revealed to them in a vision during their dream fast. Dreams were especially important in people's lives—in determining sacred songs, dances, and ceremonies. Shamans helped people to interpret their dreams and determine the responsibilities owed to the guardian spirit and what powers could be obtained from that spirit. People held their various personal charms in medicine bundles. If individuals carefully observed their duties and conducted themselves properly, their powers grew over the course of their lives. Elders thus had the greatest spiritual powers.

Shamans were believed to have special powers. Some specialized in hunting charms and love medicines. With their especially strong powers, shamans used spiritual cures to treat patients with various illnesses. Shamans also had a great knowledge of herbal medicines and great skill in treating illnesses and injuries. Many shamans belonged to the **Mitä'win**, or Medicine Lodge, which was established to ensure good health and a long life.

In the Medicine Lodge, the oldest secret religious society among the Menominee, people honored their spiritual hero, Manabush. Shamans became members through inheritance or invitation, and their initiation was highly ritualized. The Menominee believed that Manabush came among the people and helped them in many ways. He showed the Menominee shamans how to cure illness and injury, and thereafter the Mitä'win

Society was endowed with these powers. He gave them animal-skin bags that contained powerful medicine. He taught them how to use these medicines, along with songs, dances, and rituals. As taught by Manabush, the Mitä'win Society held membership rites, memorial services for deceased members, and rituals to heal the sick. However, not all of the shamans used this power for good intentions. Some separated and formed another society, called the Witches' Society, which hurt people.

Legend said that Manabush gave the Menominee drums and flutes to accompany their songs and dances. He showed them how to make fishnets. He taught the people how to be skillful hunters and warriors and endowed them with special powers to kill the bear known as O'wasso. A man hunted a bear only to ease hunger and provide winter clothing, and he offered apologies to O'wasso before making the kill. Even then, members of the Bear phratry could not eat certain parts of the bear, such as the head and paws. Manabush also showed the Menominee how to play stickball, a game that evolved into modern-day **lacrosse**, as a way of honoring him. He gave maple sap to the Menominee and tobacco to be used as a religious offering.

Other societies included the Wa'bano, whose prophets drew their powers from the Morning Star, and the Je'sako, whose members, it was believed, could return a departed soul to his body and remove a sorcerer's arrows from a patient with a sucking tube.

As part of their religious ceremonies, the Menominee also had many dances, notably the Buffalo Dance, Rain Dance, War Dance, Scalp Dance, and Harvest Dance. They held an All Animals' Dance to honor their ancestors and a Beggars' Dance at maple sugaring time. In the Dream Dance, or Drum Dance, people called upon the spirits with drums and rituals to obtain spiritual powers. Some of these ceremonies are still practiced today by the Menominee.

Telling Stories

With no written language, the Menominee passed knowledge from one generation to the next through stories. These stories, which provided lessons in life, often involved Manabush. Because he traveled widely, Menominee stories told that Manabush had many adventures—both humorous and dangerous. For

example, stories told how he helped animals by giving the kingfisher its white head and the buzzard its bare, ugly head. After providing for the Menominee's survival, it was said Manabush went away to live by himself. However, later generations of Menominee still called upon him for help. Here is one story about how Manabush

Legend has it that this rock was once a warrior who angered Manabush. It is said that when this rock crumbles away the Menominee will be extinct.

brought fire to the Menominee to cook their food and keep their lodges warm through the long winters of the north:

One day Manabush asked his grandmother, "Why don't we have fire?"

The old woman explained, "Fire is not for us. The gods never gave us any. The only place with fire is across Lake Michigan, where an old man has some."

Manabush wanted to get some fire, but his grandmother said, "That old man will never give you any fire."

However, Manabush was confident and told his grandmother, "Get some kindling ready so that we won't lose the fire that I bring home."

As Manabush departed, his grandmother was astonished to see that he had turned into a small, young rabbit, which hopped and skipped until it was lost in the distance. Manabush continued until he became tired, after which he turned himself into a fox. He ran on, changing himself from one animal shape to another whenever he became tired.

At the shore of Lake Michigan, he came to a rundown wigwam and lifted the mat over the door. There sat an impoverished old woman.

"How are you?" he called out cheerfully as he entered the wigwam and sat down. "I am looking for fire."

The old woman said, "I have no fire. The only fire is across the lake where an old man keeps it to himself."

She pointed in the direction of the old man's home and Manabush ordered a fair wind to spring up. He then became thistledown and was wafted over the water to the opposite shore. There, near the old man's lodge, he again became a baby rabbit. He also made himself look cold, wet, and miserable.

The old man lived in a mat-covered longhouse that was divided in two by a partition. On one side lived the old man and on the other lived his two beautiful daughters.

Manabush waited by the spring until the older daughter said to the other, "You better get some fresh water."

The younger girl left with a bucket. When she arrived at the spring, Manabush jumped from the bushes and startled her. But seeing that he was only a little bunny, she cried, "Aren't you the clever one!"

Dropping the bucket, she chased Manabush, but he hopped again and again. Finally, she caught him and held him in her two hands. Petting him, she said, "I'll take you home."

Tucking the little rabbit inside her dress, she fetched the water and rushed back to the lodge. She exclaimed, "Look, sister, I've caught a baby rabbit. He's shivering with cold, the poor little thing."

She put the rabbit on the floor, where he sat trembling with fright.

"Let's take him over by the fire and warm him up," suggested the older sister.

Both sisters laughed with delight.

"What are you girls doing?" the old man demanded on the other side of the partition. "I've told you time and again to keep quiet."

Lowering their voices, the two girls carried Manabush to the fire.

Their little captive soon thawed out, but when the girls wanted to hold him again, he hopped just out of reach. "Now's the time," thought Manabush, "may the door blow open and the fire blaze brightly." As the door mat rose and the fire blazed, a spark also flew onto the back of Manabush. The little rabbit jumped as if burned and shot through the door.

The girls ran after him, but they got caught in the door. When they finally got outside, their pet had vanished. "He went that way," one sister cried.

"No, this is the way he went," the other sister insisted.

The old man heard his daughters. Coming into their room, he asked, "Are you quarreling?"

"No, it's only our little rabbit," they said. "He got away."

This photo was taken on the Menominee Reservation between 1913 and 1918.

"He has stolen our fire," the old man grumbled. "Why didn't you tell me he came here?"

The girls then told him about their little pet, but he scolded them, "It was always said that Manabush would someday appear and get fire for the other side of the lake."

Manabush escaped with the spark. At the beach he again became thistledown, which the wind carried over the water. On the other side, he changed into a bunny again. He said hello to the old woman on the other side. He promised, "I'll return with fire for you, but first I must hurry to my grandmother."

He ran home as fast as his legs would carry him. He asked his grandmother, "Do you have the kindling ready?"

Although surprised to see Manabush, his grandmother said, "Here it is. Where shall we put the fire?"

"Right in the center of the lodge," he said. "And there we will always keep it."

He lit the kindling with the spark and soon the fire began to blaze.

"Now we will have fire to keep us warm," Manabush said. "We will never be lonely when we have fire."

So they sat and watched the fire until they became tired. Then Manabush got up to bring some fire to the old lady. "That is right," his grandmother said. "It is good to bring comfort to the old lady."

The old woman was very pleased to have fire and she thanked clever Manabush.

And that is how Manabush brought fire to the people.

Fun and Games

The Menominee played games not only for enjoyment but also to honor the spirits and heal the sick. They played stickball, similar to modern-day lacrosse. Only a man whose guardian spirit was a Thunderbird could call for this game to be played. In stickball games—which were usually played just once a year—the competition was fierce, as when warriors went into battle. Playing on a large field with goalposts at either end, they wielded wooden sticks with a netted cup on one end. The object was to fling a 3-inch (7.62 cm) ball made of buckskin

Artifacts from a Menominee lacrosse or stickball game

filled with deer hair at their opponents' goalpost. Once a year, women played shinny, which was similar to field hockey, in honor of the sacred sisters of the eastern sky. Like the men, they played on a large field with goalposts at either end. They used a similar ball and curved wooden sticks. The object of the game was to strike the opponent's goalpost with the ball.

The Menominee also played the bowl-and-dice game. A wooden bowl was carved with an ax and knife from a large, round maple root and carefully polished. The eight dice were made of deer antler, plum stones, or sometimes wood, one side of which was painted red and the other white or uncolored. Two players sat down opposite each other with the bowl filled with dice and counting sticks between them. The first player began a song then struck the bowl at a certain moment, and the dice flew upward. The score was determined by the number of red and white dice that were turned up. The players took turns striking the bowl until one person won all the counting sticks.

The Menominee carved and used bowls like this during maple syrup production time.

The Menominee also played the moccasin, or bullet, game. Five people took part in this game—four as players and one as drummer and singer. The players used four bullets, or balls, one of which was colored or marked in some way; four moccasins; and thirty or forty counting sticks. They also needed a blanket and a stick about 3 feet (0.9 m) long. The moccasins were placed on the blanket and the bullets were carefully hidden under them. With the stick, an opponent then flipped over the moccasin, under which painted bullets might be hidden. More points were scored for a first guess and fewer with a second guess. The game was played until one team won all the counting sticks.

A rough game, which often became an all-out fight, was called *hato'wi*, or *ato'wi*. In this game, sides were chosen or members of a friendly visiting tribe, such as the Potawatomi, competed against the Menominee. The object of the game was to determine which players could keep their temper. Each side took turns kicking an opponent in the rear as hard as possible with a moccasin-clad foot, shouting "Hato'wi!" Whenever the Menominee got together to play other sports and games, if anyone shouted, "Hato'wi!" they immediately began to play this game.

Another popular game was snow-snake, which was played during the winter. Players used a hardwood stick about 5 to 6 feet (1.5 to 1.8 m) long with a bulblike end resembling a snake's head. The player grasped the opposite end, or "tail," and skimmed the stick over the slippery ice or snow as far as possible.

Through the seasons the Menominee enjoyed these and many other games, along with footraces, wrestling, bow-shooting contests, and many other competitions.

The Milwaukee Public Museum features a display of different tribes in Wisconsin. Part of the display features this figure showing off traditional Menominee clothing.

These beliefs and practices shaped Menominee culture and helped the Menominee remain a thriving tribe as the United States became a nation. Nevertheless, in their history the Menominee have also endured hardships and difficulties that challenged their way of life and their very existence.

Jean Nicolet arrived in Wisconsin in 1634.

It is my boast that these hands are unstained by human blood.

—Chief Tomah,
Menominee chief, 1810

OVERCOMING HARDSHIPS

In the centuries after the first Menominee tribes came to Wisconsin, the group lived relatively peacefully, away from the influence of Europeans, who began sending explorers to North America in the 1400s. It was not until the 1600s that a Frenchman named Jean Nicolet was thought to have encountered the Menominee for the first time. Little did the Menominee know that this encounter, and others with various European people after, would change their culture and way of life forever.

The French Arrive

Although there is no hard evidence that the Menominee were among any of the Native people who encountered Jean Nicolet when he landed on the shores of Wisconsin in 1634, it is likely that at least some Menominee met Nicolet in his "Chinese Robe." Nicolet wore this elaborate robe because he thought that he had landed on the shores of China when he crossed Lake Michigan. Nicolet discovered Menominee villages at the mouth of the Menominee River and at La Baye, now known as Green Bay. His visit marked the beginning of the fur trade era and many changes for the Menominee.

Priests such as Jesuits came to preach to Native Americans.

In 1667, Nicolas Perrot, another French fur trader, came to the region to negotiate a peace agreement between the Menominee and the Potawatomi, who were at war over killings between their tribes. The next year, Perrot carried the first load of furs from La Baye. In 1669, Jesuit missionary Claude Allouez came to live with a small group of Menominee in a village near the bay.

He, along with Father Louis Andre, soon founded a mission on the Fox River near Oconto, Wisconsin. In 1671, the French claimed the lands of the Great Lakes region by a formal act at Sault Sainte Marie. All the Native people living there, including the Menominee, were declared French subjects. Two years later, in 1673, the legendary French explorers Louis Jolliet and Father Marquette visited the Menominee.

During the 1600s, as more missions were established and the fur trade prospered, the Menominee were tragically affected in several major ways. They quickly became dependent upon trade goods and French traders. Iron and brass tools and weapons replaced stone knives and hatchets. Women abandoned clay pots and gourds in favor of metal kettles. They also began to use steel needles and awls instead of those made of bone. Blankets and cloth replaced skins and furs in making garments.

The Menominee devoted themselves to trapping beavers and other fur-bearing animals for the traders instead of providing for themselves. In the past, they had hunted only to provide for the needs of their families and relatives. Now they had to obtain large numbers of pelts to trade for the goods that their people wanted. The hunted animals soon became scarce and the Menominee were forced to range farther from their villages. People dispersed into smaller bands, which weakened their society, especially the clans. More clans were formed and there was a major change in the organization of the clan system. Small, migrating bands now became more important than the clans and villages.

During this time, the Menominee also became involved in wars between France and England. They allied themselves with France because they had befriended the French fur traders. They remained loyal to France because the nation proclaimed sovereignty over their territory, dominating the western Great Lakes region—including Wisconsin—from 1630 to 1760. After the French and Indian War (1754–1763), the British replaced the French in Menominee territory.

Most tragically, Europeans brought diseases against which the Menominee had little or no resistance. Smallpox first struck the western Great Lakes area between 1781 and 1783 and nearly wiped out entire bands. This was the first of a series of epidemics that swept through Menominee territory. Others were to follow in later years, severely upsetting the population of Menominee.

Life in the United States

The region was ceded to the United States in 1794 as part of the Jay Treaty. However, the United States did not take an active interest in the area around the Great Lakes, which until the early nineteenth century was known as the Northwest Territory. In 1800, the Menominee lands were included in a region set aside for Native peoples.

In 1804, a Menominee man named Tomah became head chief of the Menominee, after his older brother Glode died while on a winter hunt. Glode had earlier succeeded their father, Carron, as head chief. Tomah was a leader devoted to his people. He made alliances with settlers in Wisconsin, and became so well regarded that settlers wanted to honor him by naming their town after him. To this day, Tomah remains a town in Wisconsin.

The People and Culture of the Menominee

In 1812, Oshkosh, who was to become one of the best-known Menominee chiefs, was placed under Tomah's guidance and care. There he flourished among the Menominee people. Eventually, Oshkosh would make his name in Menominee history by entering in

This statue commemorates Chief Oshkosh.

negotiations with the United States government to protect and preserve Menominee lands in the 1830s and 1840s.

In 1814, the Treaty of Ghent, which ended the War of 1812, fully granted the Great Lakes region to the United States. In 1815, the first Americans moved into the region when the United States government established a trading post and **Indian agency** at La Baye, changing the name to Green Bay. The United States soon brought more changes to the Menominee. The following year, the federal government established a fort, Indian agency, and fur factory at Green Bay. The Menominee held a council and declared their allegiance to the United States. In 1817, the first peace treaty was made between the US government and the Menominee. Tomah died the following year. At the time, the Menominee claimed about 11 million acres (4,451,542 ha) in Wisconsin and upper Michigan.

A Time for Treaties

Over the years that followed, many treaties and changes happened for the Menominee. First, they agreed on new boundaries with neighboring tribes, such as the Ojibwe, in an effort to end fighting between the tribes. Next, following much negotiation and struggle, between 1827 and 1830 the Menominee agreed to sell 500,000 acres (202,343 ha) of their lands, at four and a half cents per acre, to tribes from New York that had been displaced by warfare. These agreements became known as the Treaties of Butte des Morts. For their sale they received $20,000. The Menominee also sold an equal number of acres to the US government at five cents per acre to be paid in annuities. However, there were problems with the treaty. When the United States government went to pass it, they gave better lands to the New York Native Americans than had originally been agreed upon. This infuriated the Menominee, who were only appeased in 1832 when the government offered them $1,000 in gifts, five hundred bushels of corn, ten barrels of pork, and ten barrels of flour.

This was not the end of unrest for the Menominee, however. During the Black Hawk War in 1832, Oshkosh allied with the United States against the Sauk and Fox tribes. This was a change from his alliance with the British against the United States twenty years earlier in the War of 1812. After the Black Hawk War, Oshkosh was recognized by the federal government as head chief and spokesperson of the Menominee.

Other hardships arose soon after. The presence of US troops in Menominee territory made the Native people susceptible to diseases they had not yet encountered. One such disease was cholera. In 1834, a cholera epidemic swept through Native settlements in the Great Lakes region, killing about one in four Menominee. At about the same time (1832–1835), smallpox epidemics raged through Menominee, Winnebago, and Potawatomi settlements in Illinois and Wisconsin. Many Menominee suffered and died.

In 1836, the Wisconsin Territory was organized. In the Treaty of Cedars, the Menominee agreed to sell 4 million acres (1,618,743 ha) of their land at seventeen cents per acre to the US government. The Menominee gave up substantial land north of the Fox River and east of the Wolf River. Twelve years later, in 1848, Wisconsin became the thirtieth state in the Union. At this time the Menominee agreed to a treaty at Lake Poygan, which proposed they sell the rest of their land in Wisconsin in exchange for $350,000 and 600,000 acres (242,811 ha) of land in Minnesota. Eventually, they sold 4.5 million acres (1,821,085 ha) of their territory to the government. However, 2,500 Menominee refused to be relocated.

More challenges were yet to come. In 1849, another cholera epidemic devastated the Ojibwe and Menominee tribes. That same year, three hundred people of both Menominee and European descent accepted payments from the US government in exchange for relinquishing their tribal affiliation. People were led to believe this was the only way they could remain in their homes and not be shipped off to Crow Wing County in Minnesota.

In July 1850, Oshkosh led ten other Menominee chiefs, along with two assistants, two interpreters, and three government agents from the town of Oshkosh to Crow Wing, Minnesota. Government officials had asked the leaders to inspect the region, where the Menominee were to be granted 600,000 acres (242,811 ha). Upon their return, however, the tribal leaders declared that the government had misrepresented the land, which lacked the natural resources to support their people. The leaders also observed that there was considerable conflict among the tribes already living there. Oshkosh and the other leaders sought to amend the 1848 treaty. During negotiations, the Menominee were allowed to temporarily move into an area between the upper Wolf and Oconto Rivers in Wisconsin.

By the 1850s, Wisconsin and other Great Lakes regions were becoming popular destinations for new settlers. Native lands were sought after. As a result, the Native people were expected to leave their homelands. In September 1852, federal officials authorized the forcible removal of the Menominee from the Lake Poygan region to the area around what would become Keshena, Wisconsin, where the present-day reservation is located. However, the people were not moved until November when the ice had begun to form on the river. Since the Menominee had to travel in birch bark canoes, which were easily damaged in the icy water, the relocation proved to be a cruel hardship for families.

By 1852 all the Menominee bands had moved onto the present reservation, although they had not fully accepted the 1848 treaty. Until a final agreement was drawn up on May 12, 1854, at Keshena Falls, they operated under the terms of the 1836 Treaty of the Cedars. Under the new agreement, the Wolf River

Members of the Menominee tribe traveled to Crow Wing, Minnesota, where the tribe was meant to be relocated.

Treaty, signed by Chiefs Keshi'niu and Oshkosh, the Menominee Reservation was formally established. At the time, the reservation included twelve townships totaling 276,480 acres (111,887 ha). When the Menominee River band arrived on the reservation, most people made their homes at the "Payground," as it was popularly known. However, the place was later renamed Keshena in honor of the rising young Chief Keshi'niu.

When the scattered Menominee bands finally moved to the reservation, records noted that the people were "almost in a condition of starvation." The poor quality of government rations was especially deplorable—just pork and flour. Dishonest Indian agents, government neglect, failure of early attempts at farming, and loss of traditional hunting grounds contributed to the wretched conditions. The inadequate diet and the long period of federal neglect further weakened many tribal members and made them susceptible to disease.

The Civil War and Beyond

In 1862, the Menominee Council pledged its allegiance to the North in the Civil War. During the conflict, which raged until 1865, 120 Menominee warriors enlisted in various Wisconsin regiments and about one in three were killed. Meanwhile, a Catholic school was established in Keshena in 1863. That year, President Abraham Lincoln signed a congressional act for construction of a major road through the reservation between Fort Howard (now Green Bay) and Fort Wilkins near Marquette, Michigan. At the time, the Menominee were actively farming about 400 acres (161.9 ha) of land on the reservation. However, many Menominee were still living in poverty and the road did little to bring economic opportunity.

In 1865, a smallpox epidemic broke out among the Menominee in Keshena when a priest refused to honor a Board of Health request to promptly bury the dead. Insisting on religious services, the priest spread the disease to nearly everyone who went to the funeral. Seventy-nine people died in this epidemic. In 1869–1870, the vaccination of traders, missionaries, and federal Indian agents finally slowed the smallpox epidemics, although there were still outbreaks in some communities both on and off the reservation.

The tribe owned valuable forest lands, and in 1868, tribal leaders accused a group of unscrupulous speculators in Wisconsin, known as the "Pine Ring," of setting fires on the reservation to destroy pine stands and trying to clear cut Menominee timber. In December, eight Menominee chiefs formally protested the activities of the Pine Ring. As the great tribal leader Grizzly Bear once said, "The forest is our life, and, as you perceive, we do not like to part with it—or any of our land as we said to you before."

A congressional act of 1871 provided for the sale of tribal lands with the consent of the tribal council. However, the tribal council forbade the sale of any more land. The Secretary of the Interior agreed that the Menominee would be allowed to cut timber on their own land and sell the logs to mills located on the reservation. Later acts provided for improvement of the Wolf and Oconto Rivers to accommodate "log drives" down the rivers.

Following a very dry summer in which there was no rain from July to October in northern Wisconsin, forest fires blazed in Marinette, Oconto, Brown, Door, Kewaunee, and Shawano Counties. On October 8, 1871, the devastating Peshtigo Fire swept through the region. In just four hours, this fire killed about 1,200 people and burned a swath 10 miles (16 km) wide and 40 miles (64 km) long. Although the fire did not reach the reservation, the sites of ancient Menominee villages, including the home of the Peshtigo River band led by Shaw-won-na-pen-acce, were burned.

The following year, in 1872, Menominee leaders made a bold effort to take charge of their own forests. A tribal lumber camp was organized, operating under the supervision of the Indian agent. This camp used only Menominee labor.

In 1875, Neopit was elected head chief after his brother A'kwine'ni, who had succeeded Oshkosh as chief, was convicted and imprisoned for a crime. In 1878, the Indian Department was pressured by the Pine Ring to halt Menominee logging operations. The Menominee suffered unemployment and poverty, but tribal leaders refused to sell any of their land. Expressing the feelings of the people, Chief Neopit stated, "We will not consent to the sale of any more land. We want it for our children and grandchildren. We accepted our present reservation when it was considered of no value by our white friends. And all we ask is to be permitted to keep it as a home." Finally, in 1882, a special act of Congress permitted the Menominee to cut "dead and down" timber every year.

In 1888, the US Attorney General ordered the Menominee to cease timber cutting on the reservation, which he declared to be government property. Government officials also asked Chief Neopit to give up his title, as "there were to be Chiefs no more," and the Native Americans were to "be subject only to the USA." However, in 1890, a congressional act authorized Menominee logging on the reservation, under government supervision, of up to 20 million board feet (about 1.7 million cubic feet or 47,200 cubic meters) a year.

Life on the Reservation

After the government school in Keshena was closed due to a lack of students, small schools were established in West Branch, known as Kenepowa Settlement, and South Branch, known as Little Oconto. Menominee teachers taught lessons in both Menominee and English. In 1875, the Menominee tribal council agreed to establish a central boarding school in Keshena, with compulsory attendance. In 1881, the Keshena Day School became a government boarding school, with a new schoolhouse built in 1883. Meanwhile, in 1880, a Franciscan mission had been established in Keshena.

The People and Culture of the Menominee

A group of Menominee girls being trained to work as maids at the Tomah Indian Training School in the late 1800s

However, Catholic priests were not allowed to offer religious instruction at Keshena Day School. The Green Bay diocese then authorized a Catholic boarding school run by the Sisters of Saint Joseph of Carondolet. The Menominee agreed to support both the government boarding school and Saint Joseph Industrial School (as the Catholic school was called) financially. In 1885, the schools in West Branch and South Branch were closed, and all Menominee children on the reservation had to attend the boarding schools in Keshena.

In 1883, the federal government organized a special Native police service on the reservation with trained Menominee police officers. Soon after, a Court of Indian Offenses was established at Keshena, with three chiefs serving as judges: Neopit, Niaqtowapomi, and "Chickeny" (Ma'tshiKine'u). Menominee leaders also retained more control over their own local government when the General Allotment Act was passed in 1887. This law provided that reservation lands in the United

States be allotted, or divided, among individual tribal members. However, the Menominee wisely chose to hold all their land in common as tribal property.

In 1892, Congress authorized construction of a railroad through the reservation. The tracks crossed the Wolf River where the new town of Neopit was soon to be built. At this time, Paper Mill Dam was also constructed on the Wolf River near Shawano. However, the sturgeons could no longer reach their spawning grounds at Keshena Falls, and the Menominee lost one of their ancestral sources of food.

Between 1919 and 1920, an influenza epidemic swept through the reservation killing both young and old, including many schoolchildren in the Keshena area. Through the ensuing years, tribal leaders struggled to provide adequate health care, education, and employment opportunities for their people. Over the next three decades, they also worked to improve social, political, and economic conditions on the reservation. Despite their hardships, the Menominee are one of few Native tribes to stay on and manage a reservation close to their Native lands today.

Preserving the Language

The Menominee speak an Algonquian language similar to that spoken by many Eastern tribes. However, Menominee differs greatly from the languages spoken by other Algonquian peoples, indicating that they have long lived as a stable group in the same territory. The Menominee also used Ojibwe as a second language in speaking with others during the fur-trading era. Scholars did not begin to examine the Menominee language until the late nineteenth century.

By the 1920s, many people spoke English rather than Menominee, and usage varied widely between older and younger generations. By 1965, only three hundred to five hundred people could speak Menominee, and by the 1990s it was spoken by just a few of the oldest people. As part of an effort to save the language, children now learn to speak Menominee in school. The College of Menominee Nation also provides language lessons via their website, www.menominee.edu. There is an effort being made by many Menominee people to establish a Menominee language immersion day care and an immersion school. If begun, this school would seek to preserve the language and provide more native Menominee speakers to the Menominee tribe.

The following examples are drawn from the College of Menominee Nation. The language is complex, but the following key will help in pronunciation.

Menominee Alphabet (eighteen characters)

a ae c e h i k l m n o p q s t u w y

Vowels

ä as in saw

äë as in sat

ë as in say

ï as in see

ö as in so

ü as in sue

Vowels that do not have the umlaut (¨) over them are pronounced like the short vowels in English.

Consonants

All consonants in Menominee are pronounced the same as in English with the exceptions of c, which is always pronounced as the "ch" in *ch*urch and s, which is either pronounced as in *s*assy or as in *sh*oot. The letter *q* represents a glottal stop, which is a catch-in-the-breath sound as in "oh-oh."

Basic Conversations

Pösöh.	Hello.
Anämaehkatwan.	Greeting (with handshake).
Täq äës wïhseyan?	What is your name?
(Your name) eneq äës wïhseyan.	My name is (your name).
Täq äëkäëyan?	What are you called?
(Your name) eneq äëkäëyan.	I am called (your name).
Täq äës mamäceqtaw wïhseyan?	What is your Indian name?
(Your name) mamäceqtaw wïhseyan.	My Indian name is (your name).
Äneq näp?	How are you?
Eneq new änow.	I am fine.
Kenah taeh?	And you?
Nemäëhnow-ïm.	I am well.

Nemäënïnehtan 's kew-nian!	I am happy to see you!
Ahkanom äwew ayäckwat kës-nian.	It is a long time since I last saw you.
Menïkësekat, änow?	It is a nice day, isn't it?
Ëh, käëqc- menïkesekat yöhpeh!	Yes, it is a very nice day today!
Ïaq enakah äësïyan?	Where are you going?
Nekätaw nekëwäëm.	I am going home.
Äq nakah wäëpïyan?	Where are you coming from?
Säwanoh eneq wäëpïyan.	I am coming from Shawano.
Mäëhnow- pemätesenon yöhpeh!	Live well today!
Nekötäës mesek. kew-nian	I'll see you again sometime.
Pösöh.	Good-bye.

Throughout the centuries, the Menominee have endured much, but today they continue to be a presence in the Great Lakes region. In particular, the Menominee Nation remains significant in Wisconsin. Towns and cities have taken on popular chief names, such as Tomah and Oshkosh, a constant reminder of the importance of the Menominee Nation to Native American and Wisconsin history.

A powwow takes place in Keshena, Wisconsin, in 2007.

CHAPTER SIX

Don't give up.

—Ron Corn Jr.,
Menominee
language teacher

THE NATION'S PRESENCE NOW

After enduring hardships and facing obstacles, as well as giving up most of their ancestral lands, the Menominee adapted to their new lives. However, it was not easy. There were many more difficulties to come. Today the Menominee Nation remains an important part of Native American tradition. Over the generations, the Menominee have been blessed with strong, intelligent leadership, which has helped the tribe cope with many challenges over the past two hundred years.

Struggles and Successes

In 1951, the tribe won an $8.5 million legal judgment in a suit against the federal government for mismanagement of its timber resources. By the early 1950s, the Menominee became one of the nation's most prosperous tribes, but in 1961 the tribe was officially terminated. The reservation became a county and the tribe became a corporation. The termination was a disaster, as the tribe was forced to exhaust its cash resources to support its services. The low tax base could not support basic government services and the once self-sufficient Menominee sank into poverty. The hospital also had to be closed, and people experienced a sharp rise in health problems. In the late 1960s, the tribe was forced to sell its prime waterfront property on lakes and rivers to non-Natives.

In response to this dire situation, an organization called Determination of Rights and Unity for Menominee Shareholders (DRUMS) was formed to establish a new federal trust relationship for the tribe and promote greater tribal self-determination. In 1973, President Richard Nixon signed the Menominee Restoration Act, which returned most of the reservation to the Menominee.

Located in Menominee and Shawano Counties in Wisconsin, the Menominee Reservation today consists of about 235,500 acres (95,303 ha) of land. As of 2015, the tribe had over 8,700 members on the **tribal roll**, less than half of whom lived on the reservation. This is mainly due to lack of job opportunities, available housing, and an aging population. Since 1977, a new

The Menominee are proud of their land.

constitution and by-laws have called for an elected nine-member legislature, a tribal chair, a judiciary, and a general council.

With their abundant forests, which cover 219,000 acres (88,626 ha) of the 235,500 acres (95,303 ha) of the reservation, the Menominee have developed a major lumber industry. Moreover, they have become particularly well known and highly respected for their sustainable forestry practices. The Menominee do not clear-cut forests and they carefully replace harvested trees. They manage enormous stands of varied trees—oak, maple, basswood, beech, birch, hemlock, black spruce, tamarack, cedar, and red, white, and jack pines.

Additionally, the Menominee have established a successful casino and gaming complex, which contributes to tribal income and provides employment. The Menominee Casino and Resort hosts entertainment events throughout the year, drawing crowds of people. The Menominee are also involved in the tourism and recreational activities of the region, notably fishing and rafting on the Wolf River. Since 1993, the Menominee have maintained a successful walleye fish hatchery. Today, it continues to operate.

Environment and Education

To protect the environment of their homeland, tribal leaders have also fought to block the planned storage of nuclear waste on the reservation and a copper mine that was to be established next to the Mole Lake Chippewa Reservation in Crandon, Wisconsin. The proposed mine would have polluted the clear waters of the ancestral Wolf River that runs through the Menominee Reservation.

Moreover, the Menominee are deeply concerned with traditional culture and education. The tribe has restored the clan structure and made efforts to preserve the Menominee language. There are four schools on the reservation, where the language is taught. In 1993, the College of Menominee Nation in Keshena opened. Since then, the college had expanded and also opened a campus in Green Bay. It offers Menominee language classes and a variety of degrees, including a bachelor's degree in business administration, associate's degrees in public administration, early childhood education, and natural resources, and diplomas in electricity and welding. The campus enrolls over 600 students, 80 percent of whom belong to the Menominee tribe.

A young boy watches dancers at the Annual Winter Welcome Powwow in Keshena in 2012.

The Menominee host two annual **powwows**: the Veterans Powwow and the Annual Menominee Nation Contest Powwow. The Veterans Powwow is held over Memorial Day weekend, while the Annual Menominee Nation Contest Powwow is held in the summer. In July 2015, the tribe celebrated its forty-ninth annual Menominee Nation Contest Powwow.

Religion and Celebrations

Today the Menominee still practice their ancestral traditions and uphold their spiritual religion. While some Native Americans in the area converted to Christianity with the arrival of missionaries, others were able to resist the religion and continued practicing their own ancient beliefs. Today, religious and spiritual practices remain.

The Menominee hold ceremonies throughout the year, and often offer prayers and other dedications to their Great Spirit. One sacred gathering they have revived is the Sturgeon Ceremony. Long before the arrival of the first Europeans, the Menominee celebrated to honor this fish. Traditionally, the Sturgeon Ceremony included tobacco offerings, songs, the Fish Dance, and a feast in which people thanked the Creator for allowing the sturgeons to return to their spawning grounds. For centuries, the Menominee fished the sturgeons, which were once plentiful in the rivers and streams. They especially relied on these large fish in early spring after the maple sugar harvest. The return of the sturgeons meant that the people could replenish their food supplies, which were often nearly exhausted after the long winter.

The sturgeon was so valuable to the Menominee that during the treaty era their leaders chose the land of the present reservation in part because of the annual sturgeon migration up the Wolf River. Others thought this land was of little value, but in the eyes of the Menominee, it abounded in natural resources. They had long hunted, fished, and gathered in this part

Every year, the Menominee celebrate the spawning of the sturgeon.

of their ancestral territory. The land includes Keshena Falls, also known as Barricaded Falls, which was the traditional spawning grounds of the Lake Winnebago sturgeons—until dams were built on the Wolf River. The Menominee called these falls Namaelo Uskiwamit, which means "Sturgeon Spawning Place," or "Where Sturgeons Come Home." Here the high water after spring thaws often beats a drumming noise against the rocks. To the Menominee, this sound is the music of a mystic drum of the manitou who owns the falls. According to tribal leaders, "[W]hen this drum beats, the toads and the frogs begin their mating songs, and the sounds call the sturgeon to the pools and eddies below the cataract [at Keshena Falls]. There they formerly spawned and were then speared in large numbers, and the river at this point [the falls] was celebrated with great ceremony as a breeding place for the sturgeon."

Some tribal elders still remember sturgeon spawning activities told to them by their parents and grandparents. One elder stated, "A medicine was extracted from one of the glands of the sturgeon and was used as a healing medicine." Another elder noted, "A sturgeon was given to one of the elders and was cooked for ceremonial use at the Mitä'win ceremonies in the 1940s."

As they have for centuries, the sturgeons return to spawn every spring—but not to the traditional spawning grounds at Keshena Falls, because dams now halt the fish at Shawano. Today, to honor this tradition and mark the anticipated arrival of this important fish, the Sturgeon Feast is held. The first modern Sturgeon Feast was in 1973. In recent years, the Wisconsin Department of Natural Resources has provided the Menominee with fifteen sturgeons for the annual ceremony and feast, which gives the Menominee hope that the sturgeons may someday return to the flowing waters of the reservation. The feast features dancing, singing, and traditional Menominee foods. One of the more recent, but traditional, dances to be performed at the feast is the Fish Dance, which honors the return of the sturgeons to the area.

Along with the Sturgeon Ceremony, the Menominee now host other sacred rituals. In years past, they have held an All Animals' Dance to honor all the totem symbols. Since 1999, the Menominee tribe and the

A sturgeon dish is laid out before a forested landscape.

Menominee Language and Culture Commission have held an annual Elders Powwow. The elders recall that similar celebrations were once held every autumn. In this gathering, people have revived dances that have not been performed in many years. They have also enjoyed feasts, special events, and giveaways, including a giveaway of blankets for elders over age sixty. In 2012, College of the Menominee Nation held its tenth annual Student Powwow.

Along with these traditions and celebrations, the Menominee work hard to ensure more people are speaking the Menominee language and understanding

The Menominee Logging Camp Museum offers information and exhibits on logging in Wisconsin.

their history. By offering classes and informing the world about the Menominee language and benefits to learning, as well as being active on social media platforms such as YouTube, Facebook, and Twitter, the Menominee have begun to revive their language.

In 2015, a new casino for the Menominee tribe was suggested. It would be built in Kenosha, Wisconsin. After much upheaval with the Wisconsin government, including a march of the Menominee tribe to Madison, Wisconsin, plans for the casino were rejected. This was a blow to the Menominee community, as revenue from the building and operation of the casino would have been used partly to build an immersion day care and school.

The People and Culture of the Menominee

The Menominee Cultural Museum and the Menominee Logging Museum also seek to educate people about the language as well as the history of the nation. Information about them can be found by visiting www.menominee-nsn.gov, natow.org/tribes/menominee-nation, or the Menominee Cultural Museum or Menominee Logging Museum Facebook pages.

Over the millennia that they have been a tribe, the Menominee have demonstrated time and again their resilience and perseverance as a people. Not only have they managed to stay close to their ancestral grounds, but their name and historical figures have exerted an influence all over the state of Wisconsin. After refusing to be pushed from their territory, they have remained strong and independent in their ancestral land.

Menominee children
hold raccoon pelts
trapped by their father.

*You have a brain.
Use it!*

—Ada Elizabeth Deer,
Menominee member

FACES OF THE MENOMINEE NATION

Throughout the Menominee's long history, there have been men and women who have earned a place among the legends of the tribe. These men and women have made a mark on the Menominee Nation with their stories of bravery and defiance. Today they remain honored in society. The men and women below have helped make the Menominee Nation what it is today.

Ada Elizabeth Deer
(1935–), activist and
leader, was born and
raised in Keshena,
Wisconsin. She earned a
bachelor's degree at the
University of Wisconsin–
Madison in 1957, and
a master's degree in
social work at Columbia
University in 1961. After
graduation, she lectured
in the fields of social work
and Native American
studies at the University
of Wisconsin–Madison.

Ada Elizabeth Deer

A political activist, she worked as a Washington
lobbyist on behalf of the Menominee in the
early 1970s. From 1973 to 1976, she chaired the
Menominee Restoration Committee, which was
instrumental in restoring federal recognition for
the Menominee tribe in Wisconsin. Federal status
for the tribe had been terminated in 1961. During
the late 1970s, she was a member of the American
Indian Policy Review Commission. In 1993, she was
appointed commissioner of the Bureau of Indian
Affairs, a position she held until 1997. Deer's motto
in life is "one person can make a difference."

Grizzly Bear (Mahkeemeeteuv) (active 1830s), leader,
was known as the Grizzly Bear, although his name
Mahkeemeeteuv actually means "Bear's Oil." He was

also known by his father's name of Kaush-kau-no-naïve, which apparently does mean "Grizzly Bear." An outstanding leader and orator, he served directly under Tomah and was chosen as the Speaker for the Chiefs after Tomah's death. He was the father of Kinopoway and Wapimen, who became leaders of their own bands. He was the chief negotiator for the 1831 and 1832 treaties with the Native peoples of New York. He died in 1834.

Iometah (Fish Spawn) (circa 1772–1867), the brother of Tomah, became head war chief of the Menominee and fought as an ally of the British during the War of 1812. He was also considered a great hunter. In 1842, his band of ninety-three families was located on the Fox River at Little Chute. His name appears on all agreements except the 1854 Treaty. In 1852, he moved his band to the reservation, where he settled on the east bank of the Wolf River near the Payground, which later became known as Keshena, Wisconsin. He died in 1867.

Kinopoway

Kinopoway (Auhkanah'pah'waew; Earth Standing) (active 1820s–1850s), a band leader, went to Washington, DC, with this father's delegation in 1827. He also signed the 1831, 1848, and 1854 treaties. He lived at Prairie du Chien and after 1844 at Lake Poygan, until he moved to the West Branch settlement on the reservation in 1852. West Branch was originally called Kinopoway Settlement after him.

Komaniken (Big Wave) (active 1830s–1850s), leader, signed all the agreements with the federal government except the 1848 treaty. Little is known about Komaniken, except that he was highly respected and often referred to as "the Philosopher." Between 1836 and the tribal relocation to the reservation in 1852, he lived on the Fox River near Lake Poygan. When he moved his band to the reservation, they settled 3 miles (4.8 km) north of Keshena on the Old South Branch Road.

Neopit

Neopit ("Four in the Den") (active 1880s), Oshkosh's second son and one of the last hereditary chiefs, became head chief when his older brother was accused of a crime. He wrote the following letter to the local newspaper in 1882: "We want to sell our timber for a fair price. But we will not consent to the sale of any more land. We want it for our children and grandchildren. We accepted our present reservation when it was considered of no value … and all we ask is to be permitted to keep it as a home." Neopit refused to back down. In 1882, when a Court of Indian Offenses was established, he became one of the first judges. He died on March 23, 1913.

Niaqtowapomi ("The Most Conspicuous") (ca. 1830–1897), leader, was born in 1830 or 1831. In 1852, he moved his band on the east side of the Wolf River near Wayka Creek. He was designated as second chief when Neopit was made head chief. He also became one of the first tribal judges in 1882. He was an outstanding leader of the Medicine Lodge and was one in whom the tribe had a lot of confidence. He died on May 2, 1897.

Oshkosh (Claw; The Brave) (1795–1858), grandson of Old King and chief, was born at Old King's Village on the Fox River in Wisconsin. Often called The Brave, his name actually means "Claw." When Oshkosh was about fifteen, his grandfather placed him under the guidance of Tomah, who was head chief at the time. At the age of seventeen he fought along with Tomah and Souligny on the side of the British in the War of 1812. He helped take Fort Mackinaw, Michigan, and the following year he took part in the unsuccessful attack on Fort Stephenson, Ohio.

Oshkosh became head chief in 1827 after Tomah and his grandfather passed away. At this time, he represented his people in treaty negotiations at Butte des Morts, Wisconsin, regarding a land dispute between the Menominee and the Iroquois who wished to move into the region. He later supported the Americans in the Black Hawk War of 1832 against the Sauk and Fox. In 1842, Oshkosh and his band of 105 families lived on the upper Wisconsin River. In

1848, he signed the treaty at Lake Poygan in which the Menominee were forced to cede their lands. When the Menominee moved to the reservation in 1852, they settled on the west side of Keshena Falls. Oshkosh negotiated all the treaties, except the 1831 treaty in Washington, DC. When the Menominee delegation returned from Minnesota in 1850, it was said, "He preferred a home somewhere in Wisconsin, for the poorest region in Wisconsin was better than the Crow Wing." Oshkosh died in 1858 at his home on the Wolf River and was succeeded by his son. The city of Oshkosh, Wisconsin, is named after him.

Shawano

Shawano (South) (active 1830s–1850s), Menominee leader after whom Shawano Lake and the city of Shawano, Wisconsin, are named. He accompanied tribal delegations to Washington, DC, for treaty negotiations in 1831 and 1850. He signed both the 1831 and 1848 treaties. Members of his band are believed to have been the first people to move onto the reservation.

Souligny (Shu'nuni'u) (1783–1867), chief, was the grandson of a French trader from whom he took his name. He allied with other Menominee during the

The People and Culture of the Menominee

War of 1812. Along with Tomah and Oshkosh, he sided with the British and helped capture Fort Mackinaw, Michigan. He also fought with Shawnee chief Tecumseh at Fort Meigs, which was defended by troops under General William Henry Harrison. After the war, he remained at peace with the Americans, whom he supported in the Black Hawk War of 1832. In 1842, his band of fifty-one families lived near the Great Falls in the Wolf River. Ten years later, in 1852, he and his people moved to the reservation and settled on the west side of the Wolf near Keshena Falls. In 1855, he and Oshkosh traveled to Milwaukee and personally asked the editor of the *Milwaukee Sentinel* to publicize the tragic kidnapping of a Menominee girl by non-Natives. Souligny was always remembered as a fierce old warrior with just one eye. According to tradition, he lost his eye from an arrow shot at him by the legendary Sauk war chief Black Hawk.

Sunien (The Silver) (1827–1902), grandson of Tomah, became an important leader in the Medicine Lodge. He signed all the treaties except the 1848 agreement, although he was displeased with government offers. During one of the negotiations, he declared, "You don't expect he has come to decorate your ears with silver ear bobs? No, he comes simply to get the balance of our country! He proposed to remove us across the Mississippi." Sunien died September 16, 1902, in the community of South Branch on the reservation.

Tomah (Tomau; Thomas Carron) (ca. 1752–1818), born near present-day Green Bay, Wisconsin, was the second son of Old Carron, who was part French, and his wife, who was probably Abenaki. Although not a hereditary chief, he was chosen as head chief in a tribal council. In 1805, he met and worked as a guide for Lieutenant Zebulon Montgomery Pike. Initially, he rejected Tecumseh's plea for an alliance of tribes against the Americans who were moving into what is now the Midwest. However, he later sided with the British against the Americans in the War of 1812, as did Chief Souligny and Oshkosh. They fought at Fort Mackinaw, Michigan, and Fort Stephenson, Ohio. After the war, Tomah let the army establish a post on Menominee land in 1816. Two years later, he died at Mackinaw, where he is buried.

Although they all have their own stories, the people of the Menominee tribe are united by birth, hardship, and endurance. These people and their ancestors have persisted through the ages and will remain an important part of the history of Native Americans throughout North America.

CHRONOLOGY

1634 French explorer Jean Nicolet visits Wisconsin at La Baye (now Green Bay).

1667 French fur trader Nicolas Perrot resolves conflict between the Menominee and the Potawatomi and takes the first cargo of furs from La Baye.

1669 Jesuit missionary Claude Allouez establishes the first mission among the Menominee near Oconto, Wisconsin.

1671 The French claim the lands of the Great Lakes by a formal act at Sault Sainte Marie. All tribes of the region are declared French subjects.

1673 Louis Jolliet and Father Marquette visit the Menominee.

1754 The French and Indian War begins.

1775 The American Revolution begins.

1781–1783 Smallpox epidemic strikes throughout Great Lakes area.

1804 Tomah becomes head chief of the Menominee, after his older brother Glode dies during a winter hunt.

1812 Oshkosh is placed under Tomah's care.

1814 The Treaty of Ghent ending the War of 1812 grants western territory, including Wisconsin, to the United States.

1815 The US government establishes a trading post and Indian agency at La Baye, changing the name to Green Bay.

1816 The federal government establishes a fort, Indian agency, and fur factory at Green Bay. At a council the Menominee promise their allegiance to the United States.

1817 The first peace treaty is made between the US government and the Menominee tribe, which occupies about 11 million acres (4,451,542 ha) in what is now Wisconsin and upper Michigan.

1818 Tomah dies.

1820 Measles strike Native settlements on the St. Croix River in Wisconsin.

1827–1830 In the Treaties of Butte des Morts with the US government, the Menominee tribe agrees to sell parts of their land to eastern tribes of New York and to the government.

1832 US troops in the Black Hawk War transmit cholera to civilians fleeing Chicago and to friendly Indians.

1832–1835 Epidemics sweep through many Great Lakes Indian settlements, killing one-third to one-fourth of the Menominee and Winnebago.

1836 Wisconsin Territory is formed. In the Treaty of Cedars, the Menominee sell 4 million acres (1,618,743 ha) to the US government at 17 cents per acre. The Menominee surrender lands north of the Fox River and east of the Wolf River.

1848 In a treaty at Lake Poygan, the Menominee sell 4.5 million acres (1,821,085 ha) of ancestral lands. However, 2,500 Menominee refuse to move to Minnesota. Wisconsin becomes the thirtieth state.

1849 Cholera epidemic rages among the Ojibwe and Menominee. Three hundred people of both Menominee and European descent accept government payments in return for giving up tribal affiliation.

1850 Eleven Menominee chiefs, headed by Oshkosh, visit Crow Wing County, Minnesota, where the tribe is to be moved.

1852 On September 24, the government authorizes the forced relocation of the Menominee in the Lake Poygan area to the present reservation. The actual move does not begin until November.

1854 The Menominee Indian Reservation consisting of twelve townships and totaling 276,480 acres (111,887 ha) is established in the Treaty of Keshena Falls—the sixth Menominee treaty.

1862 The Menominee Council pledges its allegiance to the North in the Civil War. One hundred twenty Menominee warriors enlist in various Wisconsin regiments and about forty are killed.

1863 A Catholic school is established in the reservation community of Keshena. President Lincoln signs an act of Congress for construction of a road through the reservation between old Fort Howard (now Green Bay) and Fort Wilkins near Marquette, Michigan.

1865 Smallpox epidemic breaks out in Keshena when a priest refuses to abide by the Board of Health request to promptly bury the dead.

1868 A "Pine Ring" of outsiders is accused by tribal leaders of seeking to exploit Menominee timber and even of setting fires on the reservation to destroy pine stands.

1871 A congressional act provides for the sale of tribal lands with the consent of the Tribal Council. The Council refuses to sell any more land. The Secretary of the Interior agrees that the Menominee may cut timber and sell logs to mills outside the reservation.

1872 A tribal lumber camp, using only Menominee labor, is organized under the supervision of the Indian agent. The government school in Keshena is closed due to a lack of students. Small schools are started in West Branch, known as Kenepowa Settlement, and South Branch, known as Little Oconto.

1875 Neopit is elected head chief. The Menominee Council is persuaded to establish a central boarding school in Keshena.

1878 Pressured by the Pine Ring, the Indian Department orders a stop to the Menominee logging.

1880 A Franciscan mission is established in Keshena.

1881 The Keshena Day School is converted to a government boarding school.

1882 A special act of Congress allows the Menominee to annually cut "dead and down" timber.

1885 Schools in West Branch and South Branch are closed. All children have to attend the boarding schools in Keshena.

1887 The General Allotment Act (also called the Dawes Act) provides for allotment of Native reservation lands to tribal members. However, the Menominee choose to hold their reservation land in common as tribal property.

1888 The US Attorney General orders the Menominee to cease cutting timber on the reservation, since the timber is on "government property."

1890 A congressional act authorizes timber cutting by the Menominee, under supervision of government superintendents, of up to 20 million board feet (about 1.7 million cubic feet or 47,000 cubic meters) on the reservation annually.

1892 Construction of a railroad through the reservation is authorized by a special act of Congress. It is to cross the Wolf River where the new town of Neopit would soon be built. Paper Mill Dam is built on the Wolf River near Shawano and the sturgeons can no longer reach their spawning grounds at Keshena Falls. The Menominee are not able to obtain one of their hereditary sources of food.

1908 A sawmill is built at Neopit.

1919–1920 An influenza epidemic sweeps through the reservation, taking both young and old. The majority of the dead, many of whom were schoolchildren, lived in the Keshena area.

1954 Congress passes the Menominee Termination Act. It takes effect in 1961.

1973 The Menominee Termination Act is repealed.

1987 The Menominee open the first Native American gambling casino in the state of Wisconsin.

1991 The Menominee Tribal School is established.

1993 The College of Menominee Nation opens.

2013 The College of Menominee Nation celebrates twenty years.

2015 The Menominee Nation celebrates the forty-ninth Annual Nation Contest Powwow. One hundred fifty members of the Menominee Nation march to Madison, Wisconsin, in hopes of meeting with Governor Scott Walker to discuss plans to build a casino in Kenosha, Wisconsin. Plans for the casino are rejected.

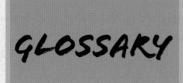

GLOSSARY

Algonquian Group, or family, of over twenty languages that is the most widespread and commonly spoken throughout North America. Many Native American tribes speak Algonquian, including the Arapaho, Cheyenne, Blackfoot, Fox, Shawnee, Abenaki, and Delaware.

Bering Strait The body of water that separates Russia and Alaska. During the last Ice Age, a land bridge across the strait allowed for migration from one continent to the other.

birch bark Thin layer of bark that may be fashioned into coverings for canoes, wigwams, and useful household items.

breechcloth A cloth or skin worn between the legs; also breechclout.

buckskin Deer hide softened by a tanning or curing process.

clan A number of families related to a common ancestor.

cradleboard A wooden board used to carry a baby.

deadfall A trap constructed so that a weighted object, such as a heavy log, falls on an animal and kills or disables it.

fasting Giving up eating food for days or weeks.

Indian agency An organization on reservation land where an official representative of the United States federal government, called and Indian agent, worked to negotiate between Native American tribes on reservations and the government.

lacrosse Modern sport based upon a popular stickball game of Native Americans living in the forest of eastern North America.

Manabush A spiritual hero who taught the Menominee how to provide for themselves.

manitou A deity or spiritual power.

Mecawetok The Menominee word for "the Great Spirit."

Mitä'win Ceremonial society, also called the Medicine Lodge, founded by Manabush to heal the sick with medicine kept in deerskin bags.

oral tradition Telling stories about the history and beliefs of people by repeating information through word of mouth.

phratry A group of clans. Menominee society was divided into five phratries, each having several clans.

powwow A modern Native American gathering featuring dancers and drum groups.

quillwork Decorative embroidery patterns created with the quills of porcupines or birds.

spawning Laying eggs.

tap To drill into a maple tree in order to get sap and make syrup.

totem A natural object or creature, usually an animal, that serves as the emblem of a clan.

tribal roll A listing of a tribe's members, including names, birth dates, and ancestors.

wampum Shell beads in strings or collars used by the peoples of eastern North America as jewelry and as symbols of good faith in treaties.

weir An underwater structure, like a fence, used for catching fish.

wigwam A domed house made of a bent branch frame covered with birch bark or mats.

BIBLIOGRAPHY

Beck, David R. M. *Siege and Survival: History of the Menominee Indians, 1634–1856*. Lincoln, NE: University of Nebraska Press, 2002.

——. *The Struggle for Self-Determination: History of the Menominee Indians Since 1854*. Lincoln, NE: University of Nebraska Press, 2007.

College of Menominee Nation. *Feather Chronicles: Fall 2014*. Keshena, WI: College of Menominee Nation, 2014.

Hill, Rick, and Teri Frazier. *Indian Nations of North America*. Washington, DC: National Geographic, 2010.

Josephy, Alvin M., Jr. *500 Nations: An Illustrated History of North American Indians*. New York: Gramercy, 2002.

Loew, Patty. *Indian Nations of Wisconsin: Histories of Endurance and Renewal*. 2nd ed. Madison, WI: Wisconsin Historical Society Press, 2013.

Lurie, Nancy Oestreich. *Wisconsin Indians*. Madison, WI: Wisconsin Historical Society Press, 2002.

Murdoch, David. *North American Indian*. Eyewitness Books. New York: DK Publishing, 2005.

Peroff, Nicholas C. *Menominee Drums: Tribal Termination and Restoration 1954–1974*. Norman, OK: University of Oklahoma Press, 2006.

Treuer, Anton. *Atlas of Indian Nations*. Washington, DC: National Geographic, 2014.

FURTHER INFORMATION

Want to know more about the Menominee? Check out these websites, videos, and organizations.

Websites

Menominee Cultural Museum

www.menominee-nsn.gov/MITW/culturalMuseum.aspx

This website gives information on the Menominee Cultural Museum, including videos of some of their exhibits.

Menominee Culture

www.mpm.edu/wirp/ICW-54.html

This website explores Menominee culture and governmental structure.

Menominee Tribe History

www.menominee-nsn.gov/mitw/aboutUs.aspx

This website describes the Menominee Tribe's history.

Videos

Discover Native Wisconsin: Menominee

www.youtube.com/watch?t=122&v=MxZ4oOFot1k

This video shows activities to do and see at the Menominee Reservation.

Living Language

www.youtube.com/watch?v=bcLPCe1t7fE

This video describes one Menominee man's desire to teach his daughter how to speak the language of his people.

Menominee March: Firsthand Look at Menominee Nation

www.youtube.com/watch?v=mstmFOr001s

This video examines the effects of the Kenosha casino decision on the Menominee Nation.

Menominee Voices: Preserving the Menominee Legacy

www.youtube.com/watch?v=J3mlyVnBmyU

This video discusses the steps being taken by Menominee members to preserve the language and culture of the Menominee people.

Organizations

College of Menominee Nation
PO Box 1179
N 172 Hwy 47-55
Keshena, WI 54135
(715) 799-5600
www.menominee.edu

Menominee Indian Tribe of Wisconsin
PO Box 910
Keshena, WI 54135
(877) 209-5866
www.menominee-nsn.gov

Milwaukee Public Museum
800 West Wells Street
Milwaukee, WI 53233
(414) 278-2702
www.mpm.edu

INDEX

Page numbers in **boldface** are illustrations.
Entries in **boldface** are glossary terms.

The People and Culture of the Menominee

Mecawetok (Creator), 10, 58, 94

medicine, 17, 27, 47, 59–60, 96

Medicine Lodge, 59, 105, 107

See also Mitä'win

Menekaunee, 21–22

Menominee Reservation, 10, 12, **30**, **65**, 78–84, 90–92, 94, 96, 103–104, 106–107

Menominee Restoration Act, 90, 102

Menominee River, 10, 21, 72, 79

Michigan, 12–13, 16–17, 22, 28, 75, 80, 105, 107–108

Minnesota, 13, 77–78, **79**, 106

missionaries, 72–73, 80, 82, 94

See also Christianity; Jesuits

Mississippi River, 16–17, 36–38, 107

Mitä'win, 59–60, 96

See also Medicine Lodge

moccasins, 32, 42, 47, **48**, 49, 68–69

Mound Builders, 12–13

Neopit, 81–84, 104–105, **104**

Niaqtowapomi, 83, 105

Nicolet, Jean, 14, **14**, 29, **70**, 71–72

Nixon, Richard, 90

Northwest Territory, 74

Ojibwe, 76–77, 84

oral tradition, 10, 12–13, 24, 61–62

Oshkosh, 75–79, **75**, 81, 87, 104–108

Perrot, Nicolas, 72

Peshtigo Fire, 81

Peshtigo River, 12, 81

phratry, 25–27, 60

Pike, Zebulon Montgomery, 108

Pine Ring, 80–81

population, 14, 25, 74, 90

Potawatomi, 68, 72, 77

powwow, **6**, **88**, 93, **93**, 96–97

ABOUT THE AUTHOR

Raymond Bial has published more than eighty books—most of them photography books—during his career. His photo-essays for children include *Corn Belt Harvest, Amish Home, Frontier Home, Shaker Home, The Underground Railroad, Portrait of a Farm Family, With Needle and Thread: A Book About Quilts, Mist Over the Mountains: Appalachia and Its People, Cajun Home,* and *Where Lincoln Walked.*

As with his other work, Bial's deep feeling for his subjects is evident in both the text and illustrations. He travels to tribal cultural centers, photographing homes, artifacts, and surroundings and learning firsthand about the national lifeways of these peoples.

The emeritus director of a small college library in the Midwest, he lives with his wife and three children in Urbana, Illinois.

OCT 1 9 2018